Keto Diet

Includes 3 Manuscripts

Book 1

intermittent fasting and ketogenic diet

Book 2

The Vegan Keto Diet Meal Plan

Book 3

Super Easy Vegetarian Keto Cookbook

By: Amy Moore

© Copyright 2020 By: Amy Moore-All rights reserved.

The content contained within this book may not be reproduced, duplicated or transmitted without direct written permission from the author or the publisher.

Under no circumstances will any blame or legal responsibility be held against the publisher, or author, for any damages, reparation, or monetary loss due to the information contained within this book, either directly or indirectly.

Legal Notice:

This book is copyright protected. It is only for personal use. You cannot amend, distribute, sell, use, quote or paraphrase any part, or the content within this book, without the consent of the author or publisher.

Disclaimer Notice:

Please note the information contained within this document is for educational and entertainment purposes only. All effort has been executed to present accurate, up to date, reliable, complete information. No warranties of any kind are declared or implied. Readers acknowledge that the author is not engaging in the rendering of legal, financial, medical or professional advice. The content within this book has been derived from various sources. Please consult a licensed professional before attempting any techniques outlined in this book.

By reading this document, the reader agrees that under no circumstances is the author responsible for any losses, direct or indirect, that are incurred as a result of the use of information contained within this document, including, but not limited to, errors, omissions, or inaccuracies.

Table Of Contents

Book 1: Intermittent-Fasting and Ketogenic-Diet

Table Of Contents 4

Introduction 11

   Why Follow This Diet 11

Chapter One: What Does Intermittent Fasting Mean? 15

   Historical Development Of Intermittent Fasting 16

   Testimonies Regarding Intermittent Fasting 20

Chapter Two: Why Intermittent Fasting Works 41

   Myths/ Misconceptions Regarding Intermittent Fasting 46

Chapter Three: What Do We Mean By Ketogenic Diet? 54

   The Historical Development Of Ketogenic Diet 57

   Testimonies Acknowledging The Efficacy Of The Ketogenic Diet 60

Chapter Four: Why The Ketogenic Diet Works 95

   Misconceptions And Wrong Thoughts About Ketogenic Diet 97

Chapter Five: Why You Should Engage In Ketogenic Diet And Intermittent Fasting For Weight Loss ... 105

Other Weight Loss Programs That You Can Replace With The Ketogenic Diet And Intermittent Fasting .. 110

Chapter Six: Benefits Of Intermittent Fasting 123

Benefits Of The Ketogenic Diet 127

Chapter Seven: Different Types And Kinds Of Intermittent Fasting 131

Different Types Of The Ketogenic Diet 139

Chapter Eight: Choosing The Perfect Intermittent Fasting For You 143

Choosing The Perfect Ketogenic Diet 148

Chapter Nine: What To Eat And Not To Eat 155

THINGS TO DO AND THINGS NOT TO DO 158

Chapter Ten: Tips On Ketogenic Diet 161

Frequently Asked Questions And Answers To Them 163

Conclusion 165

Book 2 Vegan Keto Diet Meal Plan

Introduction: 169

Combining the Ketogenic Diet with Veganism 169

Chapter 1: What Is the Ketogenic Diet 175

    How Does the Ketogenic Diet Work? 178

    Types of Ketogenic Diets 181

    The Benefits of the Keto Diet....................................186

Chapter 2: What is the Vegan Diet?........................ 191

    What Does it Mean to Be a Vegan 194

    The Benefits of Going Vegan 198

    How to Overcome Challenges as a Vegan 203

Chapter 3: Can Vegans Follow the Keto Diet Too? 211

    Keto-Vegan - A Winning Combination 213

    The Benefits of Becoming a Keto-Vegan....................216

    Tips for Following the Keto-Vegan Diet Combination 223

Chapter 4: Keto-Vegan Recipes 233

    What Types of Keto Foods Can Vegans Eat?............ 233

Conclusion: Starting Your Keto-Vegan Journey.... 269

Book 3 Super Easy Vegetarian Keto Introduction. 274

Chapter 1: Keto is the New Hero 276

What is a Keto Diet? 276

Why Choose a Keto Diet? 279

All the Wonderful Benefits of Keto Diet.....................281

The Bottom Line 282

Chapter 2: What to Eat and What Not to Eat *284*

Foods You Can Enjoy on the Keto Diet..................... 286

All the Stuff That's a No-Go...................................... 293

Chapter 3: Delicious Breakfast Recipes *297*

Soft Keto Cream Cheese Pancakes............................. 297

Keto Spice Latte Boost 298

Smooth Avocado and Kale Smoothie 300

Almond Butter Protein Smoothie 301

Blueberry and Beets Smoothie 301

Almond Muffins with Butter 302

Classic Omelet, Keto Style! 304

Protein Pancakes with a Cinnamon Twist................. 305

Green Smoothie for Detoxifying 307

Egg Muffins with Tomato and Mozzarella............... 308

Crispy Chai Waffles 309

Protein Smoothie with Creamy Chocolate 311

Vanilla and Chai Smoothie Combo 312

Protein Pancakes with Chocolate...............................312

Scrambled Eggs with Spinach and Parmesan............314

Cinnamon Waffles 315

Pumpin' Pumpkin Spice Waffles................................316

Keto Tea 318

Keto Oatmeal Cinnamon Spice 319

Keto Mexican Breakfast Fiesta....................................321

Shufflin' Breakfast Souffle 322

Cauliflower Hash Browns... 323

Chapter 4: Scrumptious Lunch Dishes................. 325

Vegetarian Taco Salad with Avocado Lime Dressing325

Egg Salad on Lettuce 327

Egg Soup 328

Spring Salad Topped with Shaved Parmesan............ 329

Spinach Cauliflower Soup... 330

Spinach and Avocado Salad with Almonds 332

Quick Chopped Salad (When You Cannot Wait)...... 333

Avocado, Lettuce, and Tomato Sandwich.................. 333

Artichoke and Spinach Casserole 335

Shaking Shakshuka! 337

Cheese and Broccoli Fritters 338

Stuffed Zucchini with Marinara 340

Cauliflower Steak Take..341

Limey Creamy Coleslaw... 343

Cauliflower Hummus 344

The Greek Wrapper 345

Egg Drop and Zucchini Soup 347

Veggie Red Curry 349

Chapter 5: Delectable Dinner Goodness................352

Baked Mushrooms, Italian Style 352

Spinach Ricotta Bake 354

White Egg Pizza.. 356

Roasted Mushrooms with Feta, Herbs, and Red Pepper 357

Eggplant Hash, The Moroccon Way 359

Falafel with Tahini Sauce 361

Asparagus Quiche 363

Mediterranean Pasta 365

Cheesy Risotto... 366

Chapter 6: Tasteful Snacks and Desserts...............369

Cauliflower with Tzatziki Dip................................... 369

Macadamia Nuts Roasted in Curry........................... 370

Chia and Coconut Pudding..371

Lemon Meringue Cookies 372

Cinnamon Bread 373

Coconut Macaroons 374

Vanilla Ice Cream with Coconut 376

Ginger Cookies **377**

Conclusion..*379*

Introduction

Why Follow This Diet

Unlike what a lot of people say about how easy it is to lose weight and stay healthy and fit, losing weight can be very difficult and hard even when one is trying so hard.

It can be especially frustrating trying to fit into the clothes one got a few years back. Even if an output costs so much, it can all go to waste if it does not fit one after a short period of time.

People have various views regarding weight loss, staying healthy and fit but it is quite difficult most of the time.

The challenge of getting fit and healthy, losing weight is quite excruciating.

One may have gone through several weight loss therapies, challenges, and so on but all seem to no avail. The reason most of the weight loss therapies are hard to stick to is because of our schedule, the type of job you have, responsibilities you carry and many other factors.

These therapies and diets have also crashed most of your energy. For example, I can't imagine myself working in a factory and I have to be on a strict diet which crashes my energy and reduces my work efficiency.

Another important reason that studies have shown that makes weight loss quite difficult is due to other failed therapies an individual has gone through. You might have engaged in some diets that failed, that is, there was no result. This is quite discouraging.

Now, what if I tell you that there is a way that weight loss can be made efficient, easy, and it would bring out active and positive results? It might be hard to believe due to previous experiences but research has shown that through intermittent fasting and the ketogenic diet, weight loss, staying healthy and fit has been made more efficient.

Research and studies have revealed that intermittent fasting has a great effect on weight and body fat loss. It also lowers the blood insulin and sugar levels. Intermittent fasting also lowers blood cholesterol, and it reduces inflammation. It has also been revealed that it activates cellular cleansing by stimulating autophagy [this discovery was awarded the 2016 Nobel Prize in medicine]. Activation of intermittent fasting prevents Alzheimer's disease and it also elongates the lifespan of an individual.

Ketogenic diet on the other hand has been proven to be better than most diets at helping people with obesity, high blood pressure, high blood sugar level, heart disease, fatty liver disease, cancer, migraines, Alzheimer's disease, Parkinson's disease, Type 2 diabetes, Type 1 diabetes, and so on. Even though you are not really at risk from any of the conditions listed above, the ketogenic diet has been said to be very helpful for you. Some of the few benefits that a vast number of people experience include better brain function, improved and good body composition, a high increase in energy, a rapid decrease in inflammation.

As you can observe, the ketogenic diet has a vast and enormous catalog of benefits, but the question is, is it any better than other diets?

Many people have had various testimonies, all attesting to the effectiveness of intermittent fasting and ketogenic fasting.

Below is a wonderful success story of a woman who dropped 50 pounds in 4 months: 'I did not feel anywhere near as bloated or sick. I felt healthier on the inside because I was not putting bad foods in my body... It has also seriously improved my anxiety and depression because I do not feel the way I used to feel before, I feel elated and wonderful.'

Having backed up the efficacy of intermittent fasting and the ketogenic diet, it should be pointed out that a doctor's prescription should be taken into attention.

Many questions come to mind like, 'what makes the ketogenic diet distinct from other diets? 'Why should it be taken seriously? 'Is the intermittent fast not another word for starvation?'

Those questions would be answered in this book.

Chapter One: What Does Intermittent Fasting Mean?

The word fasting literally means to abstain from all foods. To a layman, it could mean starvation, which is not really the exact meaning. Fasting is the process of intentional abstinence from food. It can also be the abstinence from certain types of foods due to religious beliefs.

To be fasting derives from a motive, that is, you are chasing after something. You can do it due to some certain religious beliefs. It can also be done to achieve weight loss and to stay healthy and fit. This might sound like an irony to most people. How can fasting which implies starvation keep my body fit and healthy? Well, research has shown that the act of fasting can be an advantage to the human system.

The word intermittent means occurring at time intervals. It can also mean something or activity not happening continuously or steadily.

Now, 'intermittent fasting' is the act of abstaining from food on an irregular schedule.

Intermittent fasting is a major tool for weight reduction and healthy living. Intermittent fasting is currently one of the current most popular health and fitness programs which keep one fit and healthy.

Intermittent fasting can be defined as an eating pattern that cycle between periods of fasting and eating. In this accord, it cannot be referred or said to be a diet, it is more like an eating pattern. The most common intermittent fasting routines involve daily 16-hour fasting or 24 hours fasts, twice per week.

Historical Development Of Intermittent Fasting

Fasting has been in existence for ages, it is a practice that has been carried out throughout human evolution. Ancient hunter-gatherers did not have malls, supermarkets, refrigerators, freezers for food preservation. They did not have foods that lasted year round. Sometimes they could not find anything to eat. As a result, man evolved to be able to function without foods for an extended period of time.

It can be said that there was no time in man's history that fasting was not practiced. In every written antiquity about cultures, geography, and religions, there is a cogent and important mention of fasting.

In ancient India, ancient Greece and ancient Egypt, fasting was used as a very useful tool in the curative strengthening of the spiritual cycle and spirit of man, and preventive health concerns.

In the Greek culture, contemporary fasting is totally different from the way the predecessors practiced it. In this present day, animal products are to be abstained from, while during the time of the predecessors, all foods were to be abstained from and only water was taken. It is recorded that one of the fathers of mathematics and a great philosopher Pythagoras [580-500 B.C.], systematically starved for 40 days with the conception or belief that it rapidly increases the mental perception, innovativeness, and creativity- a notion that the scientists of today have proven to be exactly and accurately true. It is also well-recorded that Pythagoras and his diligent followers were strict and adhering vegetarians.

Plato [427-347 B.C], who was a devoted follower and disciple of Socrates, had divided medicine into true and false, the true being that which gives health, which included fasting.

Hippocrates [460-357BC], the renowned father of modern medicine, was the one who invented and created the Mediterranean diet and also removed fasting from the realm of philosophy into a medical necessity. He made mention of the following concerning fasting for a sick person. Below is only a little extract: 'The addition of food should be rarer, since it is often useful to completely take it away while the patient can withstand it, until the force of the disease reaches its maturity. If the body is cleared, the more you feed it the more it will be harmed. When a patient is fed too richly, the disease is fed as well... excess is against nature.'

The primitive Greeks had made an observation that the periods by which they fast would cause the seizures of an epileptic to become less occurring and less severe. Anticonvulsant drugs were not in existence until the 1950s.

The Greeks also believed that fasting improves a person's cognitive alertness.

Fasting was also mentioned in the Bible and it had discussed the events of several 40 days concurrent fasting including those of Elijah and of Jesus.

Fasting was also in view in Islamic history; Muslims also fast from sunrise to sunset during the holy period of Ramadan. It is the best studied of the fasting periods. It is quite different from any other fasting periods in that fluids are also forbidden. They also undergo a period of mild dehydration, since eating is allowed before the sun rises and after the sun sets.

Fasting was practiced through the history of man; it evolved alongside man. Around the 14th century, fasting was duly practiced by St Catherine of Siena.

If we take a very critical look, fasting has become rapidly and increasingly practiced over the last few decades, but the question is, why the sudden change? It is what I would like to call the enlightenment; people are beginning to see that there is more to fasting than being devoted; the act of fasting has health and medical benefits.

Testimonies Regarding Intermittent Fasting

Testimonies regarding Intermittent fasting also known as IF are in various forms because people who practiced it actually saw results which were quite a surprise on their path.

We, humans, have been in the habit of practicing intermittent fasting since the dawn of time, but it has now yielded to be an incredible and very useful tool in the fitness world.

The beauty in intermittent fasting is that an individual can eat whatever he/she dims fit because it is certainly not a diet; it is an eating pattern

You can definitely be a ketogenic diet if you deem fit but it is really advisable in order to get greater results.

Some people find themselves consuming the same amount of calories with intermittent fasting or without intermittent fasting, a vast number of people observe a decrease in calorie intake, the reason being that it is easier to get full faster in a shorter period of time. Intermittent fasting is true to all, neither does it lie because some women have testified to the efficacy of its effectiveness and how it has incredibly transformed and refurbished their lives. Below are testimonies of various people on how intermittent has transformed their lives and have given them a reason to smile again:

These testimonies are taken from various websites and will be referenced as footnotes, and also at the end of the book.

A 23-year-old lady, Rachel said, "*I do a lot of comparisons photos, it keeps me motivated. It is crazy to think I have lost 63+ pounds in a number of weeks and still have 5 more months to go until my goal of one year!*"

Another lady Sharon said, "*14 weeks of intermittent fasting... 18 lbs gone.*"

Lynn said, "*I could not even smile right because I was so focused on holding it in.*"

Suma said, "*Down 56 lbs! It has been exactly one year since I started and it has been beyond life changing for me.*

In one year since adopting an intermittent fasting lifestyle, I have:

- Weight loss of 56.4 Ibs
- Went down 12% body fat
- Dropped 50.5 inches around my body
- Gone from a size 14 to 4.
- Moved from being categorized as 'obese' to 'normal weight' according to my BMI
- No more issues with sleep apnea, being pre-diabetic or high blood pressure.

So what is next for me? Now that I have hit my first big goal of losing 55 lbs, I'm excited to layer in weightlifting with intermittent fasting. My goal is to stop looking at the scale and instead focus on increasing lean muscle mass and reduce body fat."[1]

Martha said, "I loved the dress I was wearing. I thought I looked great and I actually wore it to events I was invited to. I bought the dress because I thought it was flattering for my shape and I thought it had my tummy...until I saw

---

[1] (2019)

a picture of myself that was taken.

I was pushing 76-77 kg in the picture I saw. I was big, unhealthy and very unhappy. I hid my real feelings behind that fake smile and I was an emotional eater. I was lazy and at this stage had stopped going to the gym, my diet was high in carbs and sugar. I was drinking up to 4 cans of Pepsi in a day and eating takeout a couple of times in a week. I really didn't have any plans to change my lifestyle.

What was my wakeup call? A letter from the NDSS [National Diabetes Service Scheme] reminding me that I needed to sit a diabetes test. It was my second reminder. I ignored the first one, but for some reason, reading the second reminder scared the crap out of me, I lost my father to advanced renal failure and I refused to go that road. I needed to sort my shit out and get healthy and lose weight. So I did. I have lost 8 kilos since November when I started a ketogenic lifestyle and I am motivated to lose more. I am the key to my own success. If I don't remain positive and motivated, I will go back to my old ways and I absolutely refuse to be that girl again. Do not just read my success story, become the author of your own."[2]

Stella said, "Thank God for macro counting, intermittent fasting, still a very long way to go."

Jpanzini said, "Have a long way to go still, but proud of where I came from...all thanks to intermittent fasting."

Stacy said, "Back in May I started a challenge with 15 other friends, I was 158 lbs.

The first month I lost about 3 lbs and since I was drinking and eating my face off each weekend, I was happy with that. At least the weight was going down. I was working out about 4-5 times a week. The process was so slow! Mid-August I had spent an exhausting week reading/watching/listening to everything I could learn about intermittent fasting and jumped in. I am now in my 9th week and weigh about 142. I have lost 12 lbs so far, about 1lb in a week, but I am very happy with that! This is what has happened in the last 9 weeks:

I lost 4lbs right away but still losing an average of 1lb per

---

[2] (2019)

week

I workout less. 3 times a week, maybe 4. Depends. I no longer beat myself up if I don't.

I am what they call the mix between 20/4 and "eat stop eat" I do 2-24 hour fast a week and on other days I have a 4-hour window. Saturday I enjoy breakfast and eat whatever during football till 6 pm then stops eating to get a jump on the week.

I have a ton of energy and I am getting things done. So much extra time when I am not planning out meals and have food all day long. This exists- you probably don't even know how much food weighs us down during the day

I know that while fasting behind my body is repairing itself from inside. It is not using all its energy digesting so now my body focuses on repair. So on the days I am discouraged I just keep going!

This is a lifestyle now for me. I am in it for good!

Intermittent fasting saved me."[3]

Amber said, "I began slowly gaining weight around 10 years ago. I attribute this to a time of extreme stress which caused me to quit caring for myself physically. Prior to this, I had always been what most would consider thin. It took a few years for the weight gain to become visible to others, and even then, most would not have considered it extreme. It wasn't until about 2015 that it really became noticeable.

I rationalized my weight gain, however, and consoled myself with the comparison to others. On occasion, I would encounter a picture that I was not able to throw out, and I would be confronted with the truth. I had gone from wearing sizes 4-6 to wearing 12-14's at the height of my weight gain. I had no idea how much I weighed, as my scale had broken years before and I had never replaced it.

In the summer of 2017 I made a trip to Bed Bath and Beyond and on a whim, I decided to step on one of their operating scales. Before I did, I guessed that at 5' 7.5" that my weight would be in the 160-pound range. I knew that

---

[3] (2019)

wasn't great, but in my mind, I could justify it. So, I stepped on the scale and it said 188.8 pounds. I stood in the store in front of two other women and wept.

In a moment of clarity, I decided to get it together and buy the scale. I went home and had a total pity party. "How could this happen? When did this happen?" I knew the answer to both questions. I had done all of it.

The next day I got up and resolved to fix the problem that I had created. I was the only one capable of digging myself out of the hole. I began by just watching what I ate, walking every day, and focusing on healthy fats and portion control. It wasn't long after that I began a HIIT workout three times a week. I lost weight with this approach, but an odd thing happened... I found that when I got up in the morning that I no longer wanted to eat breakfast. In fact, I resented being told that I must.

At some point on my Facebook feed, I started getting information about Intermittent Fasting from various sources. One that I remember suggesting that women should fast 12-14 hours, then have their first meal. I dabbled with that for some time and felt great doing it.

It wasn't until November of 2017 that Delay, Don't Deny: Intermittent Fasting Support showed up on my Facebook feed. I was intrigued and joined the group. Within a day or two, I had purchased the book and read it in an evening. I've never looked back since.

Starting in November I began fasting 16 hours a day. I quickly within a couple of weeks went to 19:5 and then shortly thereafter went to One Meal a Day or OMAD. It felt so natural and freeing. In the middle of December of 2017, my husband joined me in OMAD and we are still OMAD to date.

My husband has lost 30. In addition to the weight loss, both of us have a renewed lease on life and an appreciation for each other. I no longer have to pick my clothes based on what I need to cover up, but rather what I should showcase. At 48, that is a definite WIN. :) My husband has found increased endurance for his physically demanding job as a builder at 57.

Neither one of us plans on ever going back to eating as we did before.

Intermittent Fasting is now our lifestyle."[4]

Darras said, "Imagine you have to attend a party or you are invited on a family dinner and you cannot eat because you don't want to push yourself 2 weeks back by eating all those foods that you have been avoiding for months. The worst part, it is even harder to deal with people and make them realize that you are on a diet. Intermittent fasting has saved my life, I once felt dejected and sad about how I have become but thanks to intermittent fasting I feel and very optimistic about what is to come."[5]

Jeff said, "I was searching for an effective diet plan for years but I was not able to get something interesting. Maybe, my standards were high...I used different diet plans and lost some pounds but I was not satisfied until I started using intermittent fasting and keto diet. It is the single diet that helped me lose weight like crazy."[6]

Elizabeth said, "Intermittent fasting 16:8 and 24 hours for

---

[4] ("Success Stories", n.d.)
[5] ("9 Intermittent Fasting Weight Loss Before and After Pictures — WiseJug.com", n.d.)
[6] ("9 Intermittent Fasting Weight Loss Before and After Pictures — WiseJug.com", n.d.)

11 days result. It is amazing from 60kg-56kg-54kg.

The struggle is real but it is all worth it. I started with 24-hour fasting for 2 days where you only drink lots of water and no food intake. From 6 am to 6 am the following day. After 24 hour fasting, I only fast starting 9 pm until 12 pm and the remaining 1 pm to 8 pm is allotted for eating. I only eat food for the entire 8 hours."

Alex said, "I was one of those kids who could eat anything they like and still be skinny (I just grew taller instead, finally reaching 6' 4"). I was also into many sports (swimming, tennis, football). In my 20s, I cycled to work every day (over 100 miles a week), which meant putting on weight was still never an issue for me. I was used to eating what I liked and as much as I liked and still being slim, but in my 30s when my son was born, I found I was too tired to cycle in to work, I would eat sugary snacks just to pep me up for the afternoon (which of course just meant I crashed an hour later and turned to more high sugar snacks...). I slowly put on weight but then took action (no unhealthy snacking at work) and slowly lost some of it again; until, that is, my daughter was born. Again, the sleepless nights with a baby caused a bad diet, eating to stay awake at work, too tired and zero energy, and no free time to exercise. I gained several kgs. I had always been between 85 kgs and 88 kgs (187-195 lbs) but I had gone up to 93 kgs (205 lbs). Not massive, but I felt I had no control. My thighs started rubbing together as I walked: o (. I thought there was no way 'back.' I had never been on a diet in my life and everything I had heard told me that "diets don't work!" You end up weighing more. People told me that weight gain is what happens as you get older, as your metabolism slows you get the middle age spread, that's life...but that's not how I see myself, and that's not how I want to be. But what could I do?

I have a biology degree so I began to read about the biomechanics of weight loss. I read about how hard it is and why people can't stick to diets - I read lots about metabolism and sugar, ketogenic diets, and then about insulin resistance and fasting... I watched documentaries and YouTube videos, which then led me to videos about fasting and the benefits. That's when I came across intermittent fasting; I could still eat for 8 hours a day and lose weight, build muscle, heal my body, and stop the all-day sugar rollercoaster. It seemed too good to be true! I started slowly, just missing breakfast and having black coffee (Yuk!!), then having lunch at 12 and eating normally, with dinner to finish at 8 pm. In the first couple of months I had hard days and easy days but the more I did the clean fast the easier it got (and the more I learned to love black coffee).

I eat two meals a day (TMAD), usually in an 8-hour window, and sometimes as low as 5 hours. Getting the feeling of being in ketosis and knowing I am burning fat, knowing I am in control of my weight, and knowing that I am going to be eating a large satisfying meal later all felt great. I eat so well: bread, beer, pizza, chocolate, ice-cream, hamburgers, steaks, cheese, pasta, bacon! But the longer I did IF, the smaller the quantity of food I wanted, and the healthier foods seemed so much more appealing. I am now 1.5 years in, doing IF every day (well most days). I am leaner now than I have ever been in my adult life (82kg) I am in control and I love this way of eating. It's so simple and easy to apply and I even love my black coffee. I have signed up for a triathlon this August, and I am learning about being a fat adapted athlete. I am looking forward to getting older, feasting on what I want and staying in great shape with ease. It's all so simple: Delay, don't deny!"[7]

Sheila said, "It's been 4 years in the making, with a lifetime to go! I refuse to allow food to control me, obesity to paralyze me, and fear of success to stagnate me. God has placed too much purpose in me to not walk it out. Intermittent fasting saved me."

Sharon said, "I did it!!!! Today marks my 365th day of IF and the first time in my life I've had the willpower to focus on my own health and happiness.

I'm 5'9" and always been "big boned" with an obese/overweight BMI. My highest weight was 192 lbs in October 2016 and I've lost less than 20 lbs since starting IF a year ago. I've always weighed "a lot," but that doesn't make it any easier to still have a BMI in the overweight range despite my commitment to clean fasting since day 1. For many, that small amount of loss would be a reason to quit.

I've spent most of my adult life in a size 12/14 weighing a

---

[7] ("Success Stories", n.d.)

little more than I do now, give or take. I started IF wearing size 10 jeans. This past summer I bought all new clothes in a size 8. Now they are all too big. I had to buy smaller underwear for the first time in my adult life. Large t-shirts are too big on me for the first time in my adult life. That string bikini I bought as a joke...well, it's too big. I've run several races over the past few years and all my running shorts/shirts are too big. I'm just about ready to commit to size 6 jeans...but not yet. I'm no longer the girl who is "large" everything. I weigh less than what is on my driver's license...and we all know that was a lie from the start. I am no longer the "biggest" person when in a group of people. If you have been this person without fail, you know how painful that is. IF has healed some of the autoimmune aspects of my hypothyroidism. I really do look younger! THIS is why we don't quit. THIS is why we trust the process.

I truly eat whatever I want during my window. I am REALLY good at delaying, knowing I don't have to deny. During the work week, I pretty much stick to OMAD. During the weekends, I have more of a window. We went on vacation this summer where I stuck to my window and had no weight gain. We went to Disney for a week where I stuck to an extended window and had no weight gain. This holiday season was the most relaxed I've been this whole year and the couple of pounds I gained (and will lose by the end of the week) were totally worth it. This flexibility and not restricting what I eat has been what helped me be successful. I'm sure I could lose more weight with more restrictions, but I can promise you I would have quit a long time ago. Besides, people don't see my scale but they certainly see my figure. If only my face would get with the program and slim on up...

My food preferences have definitely been the biggest change since starting IF. I'm not opposed to cake and sweets but I'm not as dependent on sugar as I once was. I used to NEED something sweet after eating or I would get shaky. I struggled with hypoglycemia on a regular basis...but not once in the last 365 days, even when donating blood. I crave veggies and quality proteins. I started eating/craving real, quality cheeses for the first time in my life. The thought of wasting my one meal on fast food, boxed meals, or cheap sandwiches hurts my soul. When I do want sweets, I gravitate toward a specific taste rather than anything and everything in the pantry. Poor Little Debbie is lost without me. Despite trying everything, I haven't been able to adapt to black coffee so I open my window every day with a cup of sweet, creamy coffee as my own little "high five" for sticking with it.

I know this is long, but I hope this helps someone else stay the course. I've watched my mom diet since the day I was born. I grew up never knowing what full-fat salad dressings and non-diet sodas tasted like. I never understood why she couldn't love herself and see her own beauty in the same way I loved her and thought she was beautiful. Then I became a mom and those little punks did to my body what I did to hers. It became very hard to feel worthy or lovable. I dabbled in Weight Watchers, counted calories once, and took ONE diet pill (no thanks) but could never commit because I knew they didn't work. I'd watched my mom lose and gain and lose and gain my whole childhood. She has the willpower of steel and I knew I wouldn't be able to measure up. But this...THIS WORKS. Maybe I haven't lost a lot of weight, but I have healed a very broken body and have patched up a much-damaged soul. This was for me. I can say, without a doubt, IF has become and will remain my lifestyle."[8]

Brown said, "A lot of people ask me what workouts will help with belly fat and the answer is none. There is no specific workout that will target belly fat. Abdominal workouts are great for building muscle but fat loss comes in the form of creating a caloric budgeting or doing cardio. In order to have your abs muscles show, you must build the muscles while also shedding the fat that is covering them. Intermittent fasting rocks!"

Nicole said, "I lost 25 pounds in like 4 months. But that was with a lot of slip-ups. Like I had planned on fasting one day, and I would get invited to an office party or my roommates' parents for dinner. It is very hard for me to turn down food when someone makes it for me. But I still lost weight. Intermittent fasting really saved my life because I do not know how I could have survived."

Theusan said, "I have been on Intermittent fasting for a month or so, and have lost 2, maybe 3 pounds? I am pretty low BF already, so every pound is a bit of a battle, but I

---

[8] ("Success Stories", n.d.)

have really come to enjoy the rhythm of it, and I will probably still intermittent fasting at maintenance and maybe even through my bulk this winter. Really it just helps me enjoy my meals more and think about food less."

Gabriella said, "I've never been able to do the normal diets - eating disorder since I was a teen (binge/purge), thinking that was a great way to lose weight. For me, there were good foods and bad foods. If I ate the good ones, I was ok. If I ate anything I considered bad, I felt this overwhelming urge to get rid of it. The weight kept going up - every 5 pounds I gained, I wished I was where I'd been 5 pounds ago. I had short periods of lower weight while doing Community Theatre, nightly walking my dog and jazzercise.

I actually visited friend years ago and saw she'd lost weight - she said she ate dinner only, whatever she wanted. At the time, that just sounded crazy to me and I dismissed it - wish I'd paid better attention.[9]

I cleaned up my diet while doing some research on living on a food-stamp budget. Less eating out, more eating at

---

[9] ("Success Stories", n.d.)

home. Joined a co-op and started getting lots of fruit and vegetables to play with.

In the spring of 2015, I ran my first ever 5k and at the pre-race pasta party, Team World Vision was there and said they could take me from 5k to marathon in time for the Chicago marathon in October. For whatever reason, I believed them and signed up. I spent that summer training, along with some weight training to strengthen my legs. I thought all that running would HAVE to help me lose weight. I finished that marathon, very slowly. I only lost 10 pounds, which went right back on when I quit running.

In late 2016, I found IF (intermittent fasting) and OMAD (one meal a day). I remembered that friend I'd visited. I started in January 2017 at a weight of 172, wearing mostly size 14s.

I saw absolutely no loss per the scale for at least 3 weeks, but my belly was going away and clothes were fitting looser. I did a 72 hour fast and dropped 5 pounds, sat there for a while; another long fast with a drop, and sat there - but then my body seemed to start to learn what to do.

I generally use a 4-hour eating window but have had some

longer ones when something comes up. I don't restrict because that would make me obsess. No journaling, because that would also make me crazy.

It's now September 2017. I wobble between 146 and 148, but my body looks completely different. I'm wearing anywhere from 4s to 8s in clothes. I'm sleeping well, my skin looks better, and I have tons of energy. I had a physical recently and the doctor said all my lab tests look great - my HDL was so high it offset my high LDL.

IF and OMAD gave me back my life, a life with confidence and food freedom."[10]

---

[10] ("Success Stories", n.d.)

Chapter Two: Why Intermittent Fasting Works

It is very obvious and vividly clear that intermittent fasting is a reviving lifestyle and one of the most effective ways for weight loss, staying healthy and fit, and a whole lot of other benefits associated within.

In its simplest form, intermittent fasting is a fitness trend of eating where you put your body system through various cycles of abstaining and intentionally not eating or consuming food for a number of assigned and specified hours. Starters commonly begin with a 12-hour cycle where they permit themselves to consume or eat food from 8am to 8pm, and then they would proceed into fasting mode where they do not eat or consume any food of all manner from 8pm to 8am.

The act of intermittent fasting has received global popularity due to the enormous number of research and studies that have ascertained over time the wonderful benefits to be gained. Alongside being a very effective treatment for overweight and obesity, intermittent fasting has proven to increase and make better some health-related factors and age-associated loss of tissue function. In order for you to get a better understanding on how and why making ourselves go through such a fasting timetable is very effective for a longer lifespan and massive weight loss, I have decided to make mention of interviews that have been done with experts in the field.

According to a Harvard trained physician who is also the author of The Paleovedic Diet, Dr. Akil Palanisamy, *"intermittent fasting works primarily via three mechanisms. The primary one is hormone balance. It boosts growth hormone levels and normalizes metabolic hormones like insulin, leptin, and ghrelin. In men, it is also believed to raise testosterone. The second is fat burning. It is one of the most effective techniques for boosting metabolism and promoting the breakdown of adipose tissue. Third, it promotes autophagy, which is the process by which cells break down toxins and debris. This helps regenerate cells and has an anti-aging effect as well."*[11]

The founder of Ancient Nutrition and DrAxe.com, Dr. Josh Axe, explains further in his website that, *"the extensive research on the concept of intermittent fasting suggests it functions in two different ways to improve various facets of health. First, intermittent fasting results in lowered levels of oxidative stress to cells throughout the body. This is believed to be the mechanism behind IF's protection of the heart and brain particular, as well as its impact on lifespan."* On another note, Dr. Axe continues that, *"practicing IF improves your body's ability to deal with stress at a cellular level. Intermittent fasting activates cellular stress response pathways similar to very mild stressors, acting as mild stimulants for your body's stress response. As this occurs consistently, your body is slowly reinforced against cellular stress and is then less susceptible to cellular aging and disease development."*[12]

It is very important to note that engaging in intermittent fasting alone won't be as effective. In order to take full advantage of the effectiveness and benefits of intermittent

---

[11] ("These Experts Explain Exactly Why Intermittent Fasting Really Works", 2019)
[12] ("These Experts Explain Exactly Why Intermittent Fasting Really Works", 2019)

fasting, Dr. Chad Walding, co-founder of NativePath and The Paleo Secret, and a holistic health coach, has once said that nutrition also plays a key role in intermittent fasting. He cautions that one should not have the false belief that *"you can binge on processed, high-sugar foods and then fast make up for it. There still is no silver bullet to sustainable weight loss and holistic health. Eating an anti-inflammatory diet full of a variety of vegetables and fruits, lean proteins, and quality fats are the dietary baseline for optimal health. From there, individuals need to find what works with their own unique biological blueprint."*[13]

This declares that we should not just eat and hope to change the wrong with fasting. Good nutrition works hand in hand with intermittent fasting. You should not consume too many calories or take in high sugar edibles and hope that your fasting will redeem it.

That is a blunt NO because the outcome of such fasting will not be vivid and encouraging. So we are encouraged to also participate in a good nutritional diet (like a ketogenic diet) while engaging in intermittent fasting and there would

---

[13] ("These Experts Explain Exactly Why Intermittent Fasting Really Works", 2019)

be results that would be self-encouraging and would push to you to continue in the lifestyle.

Another view into why intermittent fasting works is that the excess weight that you want to shed in your body is stored up energy which was turned into fat. It is through the consumption of calories that energy is found, and calories are gotten from the food we eat. So you see that intermittent fasting finds a way for you to minimize the number of mind-blowing calories you eat by abstaining from food for a period of time.

During this period of not consuming calories, the body system would have no option but to use the stored energy, that is, fat, in order to go on with the day to day activities you engage in. This is a great medium of reducing the excess fat gotten from excess calories and use it for energy of the body. Therefore, no excess energy is stored up and that means no excess fat. This can be mind-blowing sometimes but it is simply one of the various ways by which intermittent fasting works in your body.

After a long series of intermittent fasting, as long as you do not eat too much or extravagantly, intermittent fasting will really help you reduce excess weight and belly fat.

Studies have shown that intermittent fasting, if properly followed, can be a very useful and powerful tool in weight loss. A review study carried out in 2014 has found out that this eating pattern [intermittent fasting] can cause 3-8% weight loss over a period of 3-24 weeks, which is quite a significant amount when compared to most weight loss studies.

This same study has revealed that people also tend to lose 4-7% of their waist circumference; this indicates a significant loss of dangerous and harmful belly fat which builds up around your organs and causes disease. Another study has shown that intermittent fasting causes less muscle loss than the more standard method of continuous calorie restriction schemes.

Myths/ Misconceptions Regarding Intermittent Fasting

There are a lot for misconceptions regarding intermittent fasting; most of these misconceptions are laughable due to their ingenuity and lack of concrete proof to back them up. I would separate the truth from fiction and ingenuity.

Intermittent fasting has received a lot of recognition from experts and enthusiasts over the years following its efficacy. This has led to a few myths and misconceptions surrounding what intermittent fasting actually dictate.

It is not an astonishing fact that the number of people who are against the intermittent fasting lifestyle is mind-blowing proportional to the people who diligently follow its dictates. There is a clear logic to this, which means there is some iota of effectiveness and sound reasoning following the intermittent fasting lifestyle's course.

Instead of praising and emphasizing the benefits of intermittent fasting, I will look at some of the unfounded myths and claims about the devastating advantage of intermittent fasting and provide a sound rebuttal to the claim that it is a wrong and unhealthy way of living.

First, it is widely believed by some people that your metabolism will increase if you eat frequently. It is quite laughable that this belief is floating around the internet. *"Eat many, small meals to stoke the metabolic flame."*

Many people have the belief that eating more meals leads to a high chance of increasing your metabolic rate, in order for your body to burn more calories overall.

I would not dispute the fact that the human body expends a certain amount of energy in digesting and using the nutrients that are in a meal. This is known as the thermic effect of food and it amounts to about 20-30% of calories for protein, 5-10% carbohydrate, 3% for fat.

Averagely, the thermic effect of food ranges up to around 10% of the total calorie intake. The main contention of this is the total number of calories that are consumed, not the number of meals that are eaten. For example, eating ten 600 calorie meals still has the same effect as eating six 1000 calories meals. It is still the same amount, which is 10%, it is still 600 calories in both cases. This is supported by various studies regarding feeding in humans, showing that decreasing or increasing of meal frequency has no effect on the total calories burned. Your total calorie intake is what matters.

It is the belief of some people that snacking and eating often and frequently is very good for the health. It is not natural for the human body to be in a constant state of being fed. When we were evolving, there were times we had to be in a state of scarcity periodically.

It has been proven that intermittent fasting induces a cellular repair process called autophagy, whereby the cells use old proteins for the purpose of energy. This process helps against many diseases like Alzheimer's disease and it has even been said to reduce the chances of cancer.

In an interview, Dr. Chaldwin said, *"The truth is that fasting from time to time has all sort of benefits for metabolic health. There are some studies that have shown that snacking, and eating very often, can have negative effects on health and raise your risk of disease."*

A study found out that, with high-calorie intake included, a diet with more frequent meals causes a higher and greater increase in liver fat, indicating that snacking may raise the risk of fatty liver disease. Also, it has been revealed that people that eat more often have a higher risk of having colorectal cancer. It is a misconception that snacking is good for the health. Various studies show that snacking is quite harmful and some other studies show that engaging in intermittent fasting from time to time has major health benefits.

A very common and widespread allegation about

intermittent fasting is that it puts the body in a mode of starvation. Can this be said to be true? According to the allegation, the act of not eating [intermittent fasting] makes the body think it is starving; therefore it shuts down its metabolism and prevents you from burning calories.

It is quite true that long-term weight loss can actually reduce the number of calories an individual burns. But this generally happens with weight loss, no matter which method you use. There is no factual evidence that pinpoints that it is only intermittent fasting it happens to because this is common with other weight loss strategies. As a matter of fact, it has been proven that intermittent fasting increases the rate of metabolism. This is due to a drastic rise in blood levels of norepinephrine, which instructs the fat cells to break down body fat and also stimulate metabolism.

It has been said that intermittent fasting is not good for people with diabetes. The belief that we need to consume food constantly in order to maintain your blood sugar level is an intermittent fasting myth that pervades the society as a whole.

A study has shown that through intermittent fasting, there has been stabilization in the blood sugar of partakers after having dinner. In a group of type 2 diabetics, there has been improved weight loss, and there have also been improved blood sugar levels.

In fact, long fasting has even been said to be able to restore insulin sensitivity in those suffering from type 2 diabetes. Also following a ketogenic diet routine judiciously has been also proven to restore insulin sensitivity as well because the better our insulin sensitivity, the less insulin our body will have to produce and this will lead to less inflammation in our body system.

This is of utmost importance because it reduces the risk of kidney failure and heart disease in people that are suffering from diabetes.

Another great thing is that for individuals that are suffering from diabetes type 1 and cannot produce their own insulin, it is very important to closely monitor blood sugar to do this right. So you see that not only has this belief been disproved, it has also been made known that intermittent fasting is very useful to people that are suffering from diabetes.

I came across a write up on a particular day that claims intermittent fasting causes muscle loss and I decided to address the issue. This is one of the myths of intermittent fasting and it is mostly originating from the fitness world. It is a misconception. It is true that the body will proceed into creating energy from the proteins in the muscles during the period of elongated calorie restriction; this is unlikely to happen during a daily intermittent fast.

As a matter of fact, a recent test showed that alternate day fasting for a period of 8 weeks stimulates fat loss on an average of 12 lbs while there is no vivid or significant loss or reduction in the muscle mass. The good news is that you can actually lose weight and also gain muscle at the same time while engaging in intermittent fasting. How is that possible? Just optimize your calorie and protein intake within your eating window. With intermittent fasting, you can still gain more muscles.

It is also believed that the brain will not get enough fuel in order to carry out activities. This is one of the common myths of intermittent fasting but it will be rebutted. It is a common belief among people that without food the brain cannot function properly. I remember when I was in elementary school, my mom would always tell me in the morning while preparing to go to school that if I do not eat, my brain would not function properly in school. Is this really true?

It has been proven not to be true. The claim says that if you are fasting, your brain cannot function properly and you will lose concentration and your memory. Not exactly. The brain does need glucose to operate. If you do not eat every few hours, your brain will not stop functioning. Even during a prolonged fast, the body can still produce what the brain will function from.

We have now examined various claims, myths and misconceptions regarding the act of intermittent fasting, which I hope have been rebutted and have been made vividly clear.

Chapter Three: What Do We Mean By Ketogenic Diet?

I know this might not really be the first time you are seeing this word, "*ketogenic*."

To understand deeply what lies beneath the word, we need to understand certain terms.

What is a diet? In the world of nutrition, a diet can be referred to as the summation of food that is consumed by a person or any other organism. This word often insinuates the use of a peculiar intake of nutrition for the purpose of health or weight management.

No disputing the fact that we humans can be described as omnivorous creatures. Each person and individual culture holds in high esteem some food preference and some food taboos. This can be due to some personal reasons and convictions or personal taste and ethics. These individual choices may be very healthy while some can be less healthy.

What is a ketogenic diet? A ketogenic diet is high fat, low carbohydrate, and adequate protein diet that in the world of medicine, was used to treat refractory epilepsy in children.

This diet urges the body to burn fats rather than burning carbohydrates contained in food which is converted to glucose, and it is then transferred around the human body, having the sole purpose of fuelling the brain, cells and all. However, if the diet has very little carbohydrates, the liver converts the fats into fatty acids and ketone bodies.

These ketone bodies pass into the brain and they replace the glucose as an energy source. A state in the human body whereby there is an elevated level of ketones in the blood is known as ketosis and this drastically reduces the rate of epileptic seizures.

Ketosis is a natural state for the human body when it is almost totally fuelled by fat. This is normal during fasting or when you are on a strict low carbohydrate diet which is also known as a ketogenic diet.

When you are experiencing ketosis, there are a lot of benefits and advantages which are related to the reduction in weight mass, performance, and health.

The word "*keto*" in ketosis is derived from "*ketones*," and as I have said earlier, ketones are from the conversion of fats and it also means small fuel molecules that are in the body.

It is an alternative fuel and energy source for the body, produced from the fats we eat and it is most significantly used when the glucose in our body is very short in supply.

These ketones are produced when you eat a very low carbohydrate diet [carbs are the main source of glucose] and a moderate amount of proteins because excess protein can also be converted to blood sugar.

This state of ketosis is very beneficial; a certain way of entering this state is through a ketogenic diet.

During the process of the ketogenic diet, the body is not supplied enough blood sugar from carbohydrate and proteins.

This will force the liver to convert the fat to fatty acids and ketones, which fuels the brain and leads to a state of ketosis.

During this state, the body switches its entire energy supply into fat and completely burns it which will lead to massive fat burn and weight loss, and the level of fat storing hormone insulin also reduces.

Studies have shown that this is very great for weight loss. You can ask that, how do I get into this ketosis? To get into ketosis, you need a low level of the fat storing hormone insulin and this can be achieved by engaging in a ketogenic diet and also adding intermittent fasting. The ketogenic diet has been proven by research and studies to treat epilepsy, acne, and it also helps in weight loss and controlling blood sugar.

The Historical Development Of Ketogenic Diet

The history of the ketogenic diet can be dated to the 1920s and 1930s. The ketogenic diet became widely known as a form of therapy for epilepsy. The ketogenic diet was developed to provide an alternative to non-mainstream fasting which has demonstrated its success as an effective epilepsy therapy. However, the ketogenic diet was later abandoned due to the invention of anticonvulsant therapies. Although, it was proven that the medication could control most cases of epilepsy, they still failed to control about 20-30% of epileptic cases especially in cases of small children and the ketogenic diet was reintroduced as a way of managing the condition.

It was in 1921 that an endocrinologist Rollin Woodyatt observed and made note that three water-soluble compounds, acetone, acetoacetate and beta hydroxybutyrate which are called ketone bodies were produced by the liver as a result of starvation or if they followed a diet which is rich in fats and low in carbohydrates.

Russell Wilder from the Mayo Clinic called this the ketogenic diet and started using it as a treatment of epilepsy in 1921.

Extended researches that were carried out in the 1960s showed that more ketones are produced by medium chain triglycerides per unit of energy because they were transferred quickly to the liver.

In 1971, Peter Huttenlocher came out with a ketogenic diet

whereby 60% of its calories were derived from medium chain triglycerides oil and more carbohydrates and protein be added compared with the original ketogenic diet. This insinuates that meals could be prepared more enjoyably by the parents for their children that have epilepsy. Many hospitals adopted the MCT diet in place of the original ketogenic diet, while some of them used the combination of the two.

The ketogenic diet received national media limelight in the United States in October 1994, when the NBC's program made mention of the case of Charlie Abrahams. The two-year-old suffered severely from epilepsy, which remained uncontrolled by the mainstream and alternative therapies.

His father Jim Abrahams found a reference to the ketogenic diet in an epilepsy guide and took Charlie to John M. Freeman at Johns Hopkins Hospital, where the therapy was continually offered. Charlie's epilepsy was drastically controlled under the ketogenic diet and his developmental progress continued.

This greatly inspired Abrahams to create the Charlie

foundation in order to improve the ketogenic diet and fund research.

There was a scientific explosion that pointed interest in the ketogenic diet. In 1997, Abrahams produced a movie, in which a young boy who was suffering from epilepsy was successfully treated by the ketogenic diet. By 2007, the ketogenic diet was made available from around 75 centers in 45 countries. The ketogenic diet was also praised and is under investigation for treating other disorders aside from epilepsy.

Testimonies Acknowledging The Efficacy Of The Ketogenic Diet

As I mentioned earlier in the historical development of the ketogenic diet, I made mention of Charlie Abrahams whose success story triggered the distribution of knowledge and the enlightenment of people to know the effectiveness of the ketogenic diet.

Many people have had several testimonies to the value and how important the ketogenic diet is. I have come across a lot of testimonies that are heart-melting, breathtaking, and make me want to take a megaphone and testify to the efficacy of the ketogenic diet around the world. In this segment, the testimonies of such people would be shared.

These testimonies are taken from various websites and will be referenced as footnotes, and also at the end of the book.

Abigail said, *"My 31-day transformation! The last few months of 2017 were rough for me. With so many life changes happening, I found myself at the corner of mental and physical exhaustion. Bottling so many inside, I let my stress take the best of me. I started to neglect my health in ways I have not done in years. I desperately needed positive change. I desperately needed myself back...*

I talk about the horrible side effects that happened to me during those 3 months of neglect and how keto diet has saved me from totally regretting how I have turned. It was very hard at first because I have already gotten used to the type of food I used to eat."[14]

A fit mom said, *"17.5 inches and I lost 23 pounds!!!*

Today is a big, big deal for me.

---

[14] ("27 Keto Diet Before-And-After Photos That Will Make Your Jaw Drop", n.d.)

I am celebrating 60 days of keto and I have lost and gained so many things!

What I have lost on keto

- 23 pounds
- 2.25 inches on arms
- 3 inches on waist
- 5.5 inches on hips
- 3.5 inches on pooch
- 1.75 inches on each thigh
- 1.5 inches on each calf.

You guys, I lost 23 pounds and more than 17.5 inches in only 60 days in ketosis

Because of having surgery only a couple of weeks into my 60-day goal, I was not even able to work out much, and so I am just now getting back into the swing of power lifting again, so almost all of this is by diet alone.

I did not count calories; I only counted my carb and stayed below 40 net carbs every day.

So what comes next?

Well first, new swimsuits. Mine are falling off, and I can see baby abs coming through, so hello two piece!

I am also sticking with keto a bit longer, because my friend is still on to lose weight for the military but after that I am going to be doing modified keto where I consume about 25 g of carbs 30 minutes before my workout for a couple of months, and then gauge if I am still losing fat and gaining muscle.

My body is an experiment right now, but worst case scenario I will be unhappy with adding in more carbs and will go back to keto."[15]

Linda said, "Hi there, my name is Linda; I have lost just over 60lbs using keto diet, started in early November, I am getting married in 2019, and looking to be my best self! My

---

[15] ("27 Keto Diet Before-And-After Photos That Will Make Your Jaw Drop", n.d.)

goal is to lose 100-110lbs total."

Natalie said, "I consumed gluten here and there...thank God I got tested for food sensitivities or I would be in poor health still. Nothing against the vegan diet, but everyone's body is different, People have had success with veganism and people who are insulin resistant haven't. So glad I found Keto, it has saved my life."[16]

A mom from Texas said, "Gosh I remember the feelings I had before I started keto...feelings of fear, feelings of being discouraged or letting myself down again...what if I fail at this like I have with every other thing I have tried for the past 12 years. Looking back a year ago on Mother's Day reflecting where I was then to where I am now not just my weight loss but also my mental state at the time. Things were better, but I was nowhere near where I am now. The weight loss and drastically changing my eating habits have all contributed and I am so thankful I made myself show up every day. So, what if? What if I never gave myself the chance? I preach believing in yourself a lot because you are

---

[16] ("27 Keto Diet Before-And-After Photos That Will Make Your Jaw Drop", n.d.)

the only one who can push yourself to make the change. Do not let the ifs hold you back. Believe in YOU. Show up for YOU. Tiptoe if you must but if it is something you want so bad... every day wake up and TAKE THAT STEP! IT IS WORTH IT. All thanks to KETO.[17]

A keto wife said, "I have been in keto for 42 days now! I have never been so happy with a diet in my life. I have lost 26 pounds, keto really saved my life. I am encouraged to keep going as I want to achieve my desired goal. Along with diet I also exercise about 3 days a week to keep a healthy life. Keto saved me."[18]

A transformed woman said, "I started my keto diet late September and I am currently still dieting. I lost 35lbs by the beginning of March. I had my daughter in January 2017. After caring for my new family, I forgot to care about myself. I forgot to keep myself healthy and happy. The keto diet and regular exercise have made me into the healthy

---

[17] ("27 Keto Diet Before-And-After Photos That Will Make Your Jaw Drop", n.d.)
[18] ("27 Keto Diet Before-And-After Photos That Will Make Your Jaw Drop", n.d.)

mom and wife and family and I deserve."[19]

Becky said, "Oh, what a difference a year makes! Keto has worked wonders for my body. Last year I weighed about 13 lbs heavier and I was running or doing cardio every day but eating tons of carbs. Now I still work out every day, but function high-fat fat diet."

Sugar said, "Happy translation Tuesday. I can honestly say a year ago, I never would have imagined surpassing my goal of a 50 lbs weight loss, but here I am 75 lbs lighter and feeling better than ever! The girl I was before was ashamed of her body and would cover it up to make sure no one would see it. The new girl I am now is confident, empowered, and strong! I feel so lucky to have a great support system around me and thank all of you who have reached out for advice or sent kind words. Keep calm and Keto on, friends.

In four days, it will be 6 months I have been on my weight loss journey with the help of keto, 31 lbs down. This has been a journey but I love every moment of it. It is not over

---

[19] ("27 Keto Diet Before-And-After Photos That Will Make Your Jaw Drop", n.d.)

yet."

Amy said, "I have been asked a lot about keto, and if I think it really works. As of today...I have lost almost 40 pounds, have a ton of energy and I am seeing a difference with my memory. This is not a diet; it is a way of life. If I can eat cheese and lose weight...count me in."[20]

Nicole wrote, "I used to be severely overweight for a period of my life. Some people have known me a long time and they have seen my progress, but some only know me now and do not know what I used to be. There are a few years of my life with zero to few pictures of me because I hated the way I looked. After getting out of a toxic relationship when I ate my feelings out of depression, I was able to lose a little bit on my own by focusing on me getting back into activities I loved which were musical theatre and overall being happy again. But I was still overweight and sort of hit a plateau, so I gave up on trying because nothing seemed to be working. It was not until October of 2016 that I learned about ketogenic lifestyle and started that way

---

[20] ("27 Keto Diet Before-And-After Photos That Will Make Your Jaw Drop", n.d.)

of eating and was able to lose 10 pounds in 2 months, just from making better food choices. In January of 2017, I began a fitness regime, going to the gym about 4-5 days a week doing a mix of weight lifting and cardio. My plan was to hit my goal weight within one year. To be honest, I did not think I was going to do it but told myself I would be happy if I got close. It has been one year since I did my first workout on my own and I am so excited to say that I did it...I hit my goal weight!!! From June 2015 to now, I have lost 76 pounds and I am a happier, healthier, and stronger version of myself than I ever was before. It is not just about the number and how I look, but I have learned that I need to take care of my body from the inside out for health reasons too. I now have more energy and I feel absolutely amazing. I finally feel like the version of myself that I always envisioned in my head. This has been a long and hard journey and there were times I thought I might give up. I am sharing this not out of vanity, but because I am just so happy that I want people to know that you can do whatever you set your mind to!!"[21]

---

[21] ("27 Keto Diet Before-And-After Photos That Will Make Your Jaw Drop", n.d.)

Salem wrote, "I did not have a problem with losing weight. The problems were with other diets that I had tried before did not account for a long-term result so I ended up always gaining back the weight that I lost. I was depressed with the way I looked, had no interest or energy, my mood was erratic. I was facing new psychological problems with phobias. I needed a solution; I wanted to turn to drugs.

I was glad and happy that I found the ketogenic diet and I was extremely doubtful and thought it was just another fad diet. I started and I was just amazed, not just the weight loss, but my mood, my emotions, my energy all came back. I was feeling as energetic and youthful as a teenager. Keto is not a diet; it is a way of life. Thank you, Keto, for how you have saved me."*[22]*

Vincent wrote, "Just before last summer my doctor told me I had to lose weight, again. At that time I was 94 kg. My non-alcoholic fatty liver disease had returned. It had improved by losing weight the last time. But after slimming once again I regained the lost weight and the fatty liver came back. My iron was out of limits. The doctor gave me

---

[22] (Åkesson & Dr. Andreas Eenfeldt, 2018)

a summary table of the calories from different foods. The message I got was that I should reduce the amount of calories that I was eating. It is a nice doctor, but he has no idea about nutrition, obviously. Anyway, I started to eat less again. I also increased the amount of exercise I was doing, spending at least half an hour every day on the exercise bike. Instinctively, I eliminated bread and pasta from my diet and I started eating very little, about 1200 calories per day. I was often hungry, but I have willpower. I used a ketogenic diet to control what I was eating. I began to see tremendous changes, changes that have not happened in a long time. All thanks to the keto diet."

Vivian said during an interview, "Here is one that I do not know if you have heard of before with ketogenic lifestyle, my warts of many years are falling off. Literally, I am thrilled. I have a few more that are starting to change and will apparently be leaving soon. I have only been doing the ketogenic diet for about 7 weeks now: I have lost 8 lbs easily. It just seemed to melt off into the 2nd/3rd week. I feel more grounded and centered, not flighty and spacey, foggy-headed. I am more peaceful and calm. My poops are great now. This is an important part, lady. I used to have major digestive issues and constipation but in my second and third week, everything changed. My belly bloat was gone. I have always had blood sugar issues since a child and now, with the way I am eating, I do not have it. I am still learning more through this journey and I am pleased. I highly recommend it to anyone. I have had people asking what I am doing. I am radiant and healthy looking than ever. I started telling them about keto. All thanks to keto."[23]

Katie also wrote that "I have been on keto since July of this year:

- 18 pounds lost
- 4 inches lost off my waist, 4 inches lost off my hips
- Down three sizes
- Down 3.5 percentage points in body fat
- Shaved a minute off of my mile time

---

[23] ("Keto Success Stories", n.d.)

- No longer pre-diabetic
- Periods regular for the first time in my life
- Not a single migraine since starting
- My skin looks ten years younger
- No more issues with sugar blood spikes and crashes, which has gone a long way in helping manage my depressions without medications
- Increased energy and mental clarity[24]

Christine who has gone through a total transformation wrote and said, "I never in a million years thought that I would share my story, but after a very emotional weekend looking at one of my year old picture and lots of encouragement.

That picture is one year apart from a very unhealthy, metabolically sick 49-year-old transformed to a healthy, energetic 50-year-old. I am completely blown away by the

---

[24] ("Keto Success Stories", n.d.)

changes.

In October 2016, I had been on a quitting sugar journey for a few months and had successfully given up the white, sweet stuff. Desserts, cookies, and packaged foods were no longer part of my diet but were resulting in a very slow weight loss. I started this journey to lose weight, and to reverse metabolic syndrome, fatty liver, insulin resistance, and if I was very lucky, sleep apnoea.

I was complaining about the slow loss to a friend and she asked me if I was familiar with ketogenic fasting. I had never heard of the keto way of eating. On that day, January 13, 2017, I came home and secured the internet for information. January 13, 2017, was the last day I ate potatoes, bread, and pasta. Those were the final high carbohydrate foods that I kicked to the curb and as a result, I had excellent results with weight loss. Because I had already quit sugar, there was little difficulty or withdrawal. I am pretty sure I entered ketosis state within a week of ditching those high starchy carbohydrates.

Nine months on the ketogenic and intermittent fasting journey, I have dropped over 80lbs and I am so very close to a healthy weight. I have also lost: daily headaches, monthly migraines, cystic acne, ovarian cysts, lethargic afternoons and evenings, joint pain, inflammation, and best of all, sleep apnoea. I no longer have to use a CPAP machine (confirmed with another sleep test that my obstructive sleep apnoea is gone). I have gained: a renewed joy for life, more energy than I know what to do with, a new appreciation for real food and cooking, shopping in regular size shops, improved self-esteem!

Turning fifty has been the best thing that has ever happened to me because it really lit a fire in caring for my personal health. My biggest challenge was letting go of potato chips but repeating a question to myself as to what those would do to my insulin response, I was able to break that addiction and have no desire for those foods that obviously make me sick.

My biggest regret is not knowing about this way of life earlier, but I truly believe God's hand was in this journey with me every step of the way making it easy to adopt this new lifestyle to stick with it 100%. I am so very grateful for real food and ketogenic diet; it has truly given me the gift of life to enjoy with my family and friends for many years to come. Here is to the next 50 years! Thanks to keto diet!!!"

Six months ago, I had my annual visit with my primary care provider of twenty years. My knees hurt, and I was 30 pounds (14 kg) overweight, confirmed by my BMI. My cholesterol was 282 mg/dl, my "bad" cholesterol was high, my "good" cholesterol and triglycerides could have been better, but my calculated VLDL was OK.[25]

Beatrice said, "For the knee pain, my PCP added "osteoarthritis" to my problem list. For the elevated cholesterol, she recommended exercise and a low-fat diet, a trope which she has sung to me for two decades.

"Fine," I thought. "But my knee pain is the problem that is bothering me the most. It is not only limiting my ability to exercise, but it is limiting my daily activities. And you, knowing by my report that I am not ready to contemplate knee replacements, have essentially told me to 'live with it.'

It seemed to me that my first-line effort to deal with my knee pain should be weight loss. About a week after I saw

---

[25] (Åkesson & Dr. Andreas Eenfeldt, 2019)

my doctor, I stumbled across www.dietdoctor.com. I read the scientific studies regarding low-carbohydrate, high-fat diets on www.dietdoctor.com and in medical journals. I emailed my doctor and reiterated that what concerned me the most was my limited mobility due to my knee pain. I told her my plan: "I am going to try a ketogenic diet for six months and recheck my lipids at that time. If I lose weight, and my knees stop hurting, but my lipids get worse, I will take a stating." Her response: "Well, that is an interesting approach."

Six months into a low-carbohydrate, high-fat diet that probably doesn't quite make it to ketogenic most of the time, I have lost 28 pounds (13 kg). My BMI is normal. I lost 6" (15 cm) around my waist, and I have gone down four pants sizes. Most importantly, my knee pain is much, much better. I checked my lipids at a free screening offered by a local pharmacy: My total cholesterol, triglycerides, and "bad" cholesterol were all DOWN from six months ago. My "good" cholesterol was UP. I feel great and feel wholly vindicated in my "interesting approach."

For me, a low-carbohydrate, high-fat diet has been easy to follow. I knew I couldn't face recording carbohydrates after decades of off-and-on meticulous food record-keeping that calorie in-calorie out dieting entails.

I like coffee, it does not give me heartburn or palpitations, and I have the leisure to sleep late and drink multiple cups in the morning. So, instead of breakfast, I enjoy two or three cups of coffee with heavy cream in the morning while I check my email, social media, plan my day, do my household chores, etc. At about 10 or 11, I am hungry enough to eat, so I'll have a "brunch" of bacon and eggs or smoked salmon or ham, and fresh mozzarella cheese with avocado and maybe some sliced tomato. By then I am tired of coffee, so for a beverage, I have water (still or sparkling) or a glass of unsweetened coconut milk. I am not hungry again until dinner, which I prepare using one of the www.dietdoctor.com recipes or a low-carbohydrate adaptation of one of our family favourites.

Dining out is relatively simple: I have grilled meat or fish and double vegetables instead of the offered starch plus vegetables. If the only option is burgers, I ask for one without the bun or remove the bun when the burger is served. At first, I had to ask the server to take away the table bread; now I just ignore it. I also make it a point to eat a zero-carbohydrate snack before I dine out so that the table bread is less tempting. I have never been much of an evening snack eater, but I do enjoy a glass or two of white wine in the evening. Lately, though, I enjoy that less (I have found that I feel its adverse effects much more now, and much more quickly) and will skip that in favour of sparkling water or homemade eggnog (pasteurized eggs, heavy cream, water, and no sugar or artificial sweetener).

My current dilemma is what to do now that I have achieved my goals of weight loss and decreased knee pain. I am concerned that if I get even a little bit liberal with my carbohydrates, I will reactivate some triggers that will derail a sustained low-carbohydrate high-fat lifestyle. For now, I plan to continue eating as I have been for the past six months and reassess if my weight gets too low. That, for sure, would be a problem that would be a joy to tackle!"[26]

Rachael wrote, "Hi, this is my story, it's long but hey, I'm 62 years young. I am writing this story for myself, so I can be accountable to myself.

---

[26] (Åkesson & Dr. Andreas Eenfeldt, 2019)

I can't even begin to tell you how many diets I have been on since elementary school.

I was a very sick kid until I was 5 when I got my tonsils out. My parents feed me milkshakes and ice cream most of the time. Well, let me tell you, once I was better, they gave me all the things I had missed! Both my parents were obese, and to top it off, we're Jewish, you know what that means. I had the typical Jewish grandmother who wants you to eat all the time or you'll starve. I became the fat kid in the family.

My parents divorced when I was 3, my mom was young and fed us what she could afford, which was potatoes, rice, and pasta. Need I say more? My mom lost her weight and didn't want me to go thru what she did as a child. I started with yo-yo dieting young.

My sisters didn't have a weight problem, so we always had junk food in our house (I became a closet eater). My mom would take me to doctors and they would always put me on a diet. I would always gain the weight back. By the time I was in high school I was probably 50 pounds (23 kg) overweight.

Believe it or not, when I was 21 there was an article in Cosmopolitan magazine called "Fasting the Ultimate Diet" and of course I had to try it. I fasted for 42 days while I was a cook on a fast food truck (first one off the assembly line, 43 years ago), and smoked two packs of cigarettes a day. I lost around 50 pounds (23 kg) and then got pregnant with my first son. So, I had to start eating and quit smoking ASAP. Well, you can imagine the outcome of that. Gained all the weight I lost back, plus an extra 35 pounds (16 kg). My excuse was I was eating for two, but when he was born, I only lost ten pounds (5 kg). I never lost the weight and got pregnant again with my second son. I gained 50 more pounds (23 kg) with him. So, between both of them, I gained 130 pounds (59 kg)!

When my second son was 10 months old, I was waiting to get on a program through the hospital called Medifast. It was a liquid diet that they monitored once a week with blood tests and weekly classes on food and nutrition. I went in for the initial tests, but the whole time my stomach was bothering me. When I got home, I was very sick with stabbing pains in my gut. I ended up going to the hospital and staying for a bunch of tests. They did exploratory surgery and I had pancreatitis. My whole system was poisoned, and the Doctor told me if I hadn't gone to the hospital when I did I probably would have died. I was in there for three weeks. For the first time in my life, they did not want me to lose any weight and to let my body heal for 6 months. My weight in the hospital was 297 lbs (134 kg).

I waited for six months and then started the Medifast program at the hospital. I lost 98 pounds (44 kg) in four months (not one bite of food, all liquid shakes.) Then I ate some BBQ chicken and the diet was over for me. I never could get back on the fast.

Then my sister got married and I was her Maid of Honor. I wore a gorgeous dress, and everyone thought I looked beautiful. Eight months later my sister died of a drug overdose. I was so crushed and mad, all I did was eat. I gained all my weight back, plus some.

For the next nine years, I went on many diets and would lose weight just to gain it back again. In 1991 I ended up in the hospital with a herniated disk in my neck. I had to have emergency surgery 5 days before Christmas. Because they had waited so long to operate, my left side was going numb down to my knee.

Then in 1992, I went through a divorce and lost 75 pounds (34 kg) and moved to Las Vegas to start over, and to be with all my family. My boys were 14 and 16 and they were a handful. As a single mom and a full-time manicurist, my life was busy, and I managed to get down to about 175 pounds (79 kg) and I felt pretty good about myself.

I was still heavy but felt I could live at this weight and be happy. I lived in Vegas for a year before I met my current husband. When we split for a while, I lost another 30 pounds (14 kg). Of course, that was starving me yet again. Which all of you know is the reason we gain the weight back. I couldn't continue this way of eating forever because I was hungry all the time. I am a nail tech, had a full clientele and no time to eat regular meals. We always had a ton of snacks around the beauty shop, so I would snack all day.

I got married and we moved back to Southern California and I couldn't get my nail license reinstated. I was home all day with nothing to do and ate out of boredom. In those three years of living there, I gained weight and then lost it, only to gain it back again. I never went above 198 pounds (90 kg). That is where I always started dieting; because I promised I would never get over 200 pounds (91 kg) again.

In 2002 we moved to Oregon where my husband was retired and wanted to have a small farm. I, on the other hand, decided to get my nail license and go back to work. I am a city girl who loves people and wanted to meet people in my new town. I figured the best way to meet people when you don't have kids growing up, is to go to work. I love doing nails.

Then in 2003, I had another major back surgery, on my lower back. So I tried to lose weight after that because my doctor said I had the back of an 80-year-old woman. So I went on another diet to give my back some relief. But, when you work in a beauty shop, there are always sweets and people bring in lots of baked goods. You guessed it – I ate. So for 12 years, the weight went up and down just about every two years. I have tried diets that were so crazy that now I can't even believe it.

Then in 2014, I was down to 155 pounds (70 lbs), but my back got so bad I was having spasms all the time. I was bent over on my right side because I had severe scoliosis. I had another back surgery in Sept of 2014. My whole back is now fused together with screws and rods. I decided to retire, except for a few clients I see out of my house. Well, within two years of being home I was back up to 197 pounds (89 kg) and had a doctor's appointment in December 2016. My doctor told me I was pre-diabetic, which didn't surprise me. My dad's side of the family all had diabetes or died from complications from diabetes. My mother had hypoglycemia most of her life. I had been tested for diabetes since I was in grade school.

I told my doctor I just didn't have any more willpower, so she told me about the ketogenic diet. In the last month of 2016, I read everything I could get my hands about this way of eating.

I was ready to start on Jan 3, 2017. It wasn't easy the first month but I never (even to this day) have eaten anything that wasn't on the plan. I keep things simple. I lost 14 pounds (6 kg) the first month, and then I stopped losing for 2 months. I didn't get discouraged because I had abused my body for so many years that I figured I was adjusting to this way of eating. I went back to the Doctor six months after I started, and she was so happy with me. My blood sugar was down to 75 mg/dl (4.2 mmol/L) and I had lost around 40 pounds (18 kg). I got off my 62 pounds (28 kg) and am down to my goal weight of 135 pounds (61 kg). I have found a new way to love and honor my body through the ketogenic diet and will eat this way for the rest of my life."[27]

Abigail wrote, "I received these before and after pictures from a friend last night as she could hardly believe the changes I have made in exactly one year. I started my journey in February 2017 and didn't take any "before" pictures because I couldn't stand to see myself in the mirror, but also because I didn't believe that I would stick with anything long enough to take a meaningful "after" photo.

I had no motivation, no dedication, and was getting very close to settling for being overweight and unhappy.

I turned 39 in February 2017 and was the heaviest I had ever been. I was so depressed, tired, suffered from panic

---

[27] (Åkesson & Dr. Andreas Eenfeldt, 2019)

anxiety attacks, and I was living my life on autopilot just going through the motions. I had to buy bigger clothes and when I wasn't working I was sleeping my life away. I had no motivation, no dedication, and was getting very close to settling for being overweight and unhappy. I had chronic hip and lower back pain that lead me to the chiropractor's office at least once per month. I was having terrible menstrual cycles that caused me to be extremely anemic and had to start taking a mega dose of iron every day.

Something about knocking on 40's door ignited a tiny spark in me, though. For my 39th birthday, I joined the gym that my best friend had bought the month before and I started a blind fitness quest. I had no plan, no goal, but I thought if I started working out to the point of pain every day that I would magically become a healthier person. I was so wrong. I decided I was going to be a runner and alternate cardio with heavy lifting. One month after being dedicated to the gym every day, I had shin splints that were so severe that the pain made me physically ill. I had such extreme pain in my left shoulder from improper lifting form and lifting too heavy that I could barely sleep. All of this hard work, no changes in my diet and I hadn't lost one pound in a month. I was so discouraged. I went from running on the treadmill to using the elliptical and started working out with my best friend who is also a trainer. Changing up my cardio and learning proper weightlifting techniques definitely helped, and I lost about five pounds (2.5 kg).

I went off of sugar, cold turkey the day I started the keto lifestyle.

Fast forward to October 2017. My best friend had been living in ketosis for two years and gave me some information to look into after I had voiced frustration with my inability to lose weight. Sunday, October 8th, 2017 was the first day of my two-week trial run with the ketogenic diet meal plan. This is when the game changed completely, and I started getting my life back. I had lost seven pounds (3 kg) at the end of the first week and six pounds (2.5 kg) at the end of week two. I was totally motivated and excited for more! I loved the meals that I was making and I didn't miss the sugar! I went off of sugar cold turkey the day I started the keto lifestyle.

There was only one problem: I had no endurance for

cardio and couldn't do more than ten minutes on the elliptical. I couldn't lift heavy and felt like I had lost all of my strength. I just could not lift weights the first three weeks on keto. I couldn't understand what was happening! I was sleeping better at night, I had a much clearer head and was much more efficient at work, but I could not keep up in the gym. I read up on keto flu and the changes you might feel during the time of transitioning carb fuel to fat fuel and vowed to stick with it, making sure I was drinking LOTS of water and getting plenty of earthy mineral salt. I abandoned my cardio and weights routine and started taking a yoga class twice a week and completely fell in love with yoga. Amazingly, I kept losing a couple of pounds a week WITHOUT all that gym time! In November 2017 I added back a bit of cardio and weights and lo and behold my stamina was back! Not only was it back, but it was even more than before. I had made it over that hump and I felt incredible.

I feel better than I have EVER felt in my life

With the help of my friend and her gym I began my yoga instructor certification in December 2017 and was certified to teach in March 2018. Now, yoga is the only workout I do regularly besides walking my dogs daily. I haven't lifted weights, nor done that excruciating 30-45 minutes of the elliptical since December. I have lost a total of THIRTY POUNDS (14 kg) since October 8th, 2017. I weigh what I weighed at 19 years old and I turned 40 four months ago. The weight loss isn't my greatest accomplishment with keto though. My trophies are that I haven't had to see the chiropractor since October 2017. I have ZERO hip or lower-back pain! I am no longer anemic and don't take those nasty iron tabs anymore. I haven't had a single panic attack and other than that occasional rough day we all have sometimes, I have no feelings of depression! I don't nap anymore because I just don't need the sleep that I used to need. I feel better than I have EVER felt in my life. Every single day feels hopeful and full of promise. Thanks so much, keto diet."*[28]*

Carmella wrote, "What an amazing year it has been for me. My infant granddaughter (an identical twin) came through open heart surgery like a trooper. It was a miracle for us!

Then there was the revelation that I needed to do

---

[28] (Åkesson & Dr. Andreas Eenfeldt, 2019)

something about my weight. While I did not have any medical conditions diagnosed, I was just not feeling my best. These thoughts were in my mind daily… today was the day I would be good and not eat anything that might add on the pounds. The day would go on, and I would inevitably lose my willpower and eat everything in sight… Ughhhh.

I had been on several diet programs all through my 57 years, and while I may have lost some weight, it was always a struggle… and I always called it a 'diet.' I just could not keep it off. A colleague mentioned that Dr. Douglas Bishop & Associates in my city, Ottawa, Canada, had helped her lose weight and thought I should go and see them. At the beginning of February 2017, I booked my first appointment to meet Dr. Bishop, and, after a body scan and assessment by Dr. Bishop, he suggested that we try LCHF. He told me that many of his patients were doing very well with this program.

I remember sitting down with Maureen, a nurse, and my weight management counsellor, to go over the program. Well, she made it seem that I could do this, so, I would try! There were fantastic videos that helped me master the stages of LCHF and keto.

The first couple of weeks my stomach didn't like it very much, but I pushed through it. I had no idea the amount of sugar and sugar-related foods that I had previously been eating. By the time my body converted to fat burning, I was on a roll, and losing rolls at that!

There were very few weeks where I did not lose, but I persevered and the fat kept coming off. I took clothes out of my closet daily that no longer fit. I would definitely need a new wardrobe…Yes!!!

I have never mentioned willpower since because I don't think about food the same way now. I have moved more into keto as the year has progressed and really follow that old saying… I eat to live, not live to eat. I watched some videos about intermittent fasting and now fast on a regular basis, even testing 24-hour fasts at least once per week. I could never have considered fasting before, but now it seems to go hand in hand with how I am eating and living. I found yoga to be a fantastic way to reshape my body as I continue to lose fat.

My journey in the last year has seen me lose 50 pounds (23

kg), and I am close to my desired goal weight, but more than that, what I always saw myself to be. I have more energy, feel better about how I look in my clothes, and, to sum it up, I feel fantastic. My husband Greg has been so supportive and does eat LCHF most of the time. My colleagues at work and friends and family are always asking me questions about how I have done it. It's simple, go to the Diet Doctor.com site and you too can see how it can be done, and find a doctor in your area that also supports the LCHF and keto lifestyle. Having this support makes it possible to be successful. In my office alone, I have 7 colleagues that are currently doing a variety of LCHF/keto eating plans. We share recipes and ideas as to how we can convert regular foods to keto.

How I eat

I am 57 years old Bank Manager and live in Ottawa, Canada. I do intermittently fast most days and eat between noon and 8pm. About once a week, I will do a 24-hour fast and will have black coffee, broth, and water to sustain me throughout the day. This is becoming easier as I do it more often, especially if I am busy at work. The time passes and I don't even realize I have not eaten.

A couple of times a week I will eat breakfast and that would be a typical bacon and egg breakfast. Lunch is often a chicken Caesar salad that we had for dinner the previous night. As I love to go to yoga after working at the bank all day and having my meat and veggies ready to cook, makes it so much easier to ensure I stay on track. Also, I try to ensure that I have some cold cuts like roast beef, pre-cooked chicken or olives, and cheese, to make a quick dinner if I don't have time to cook.

If I go out for dinner I will often order a deconstructed burger with bacon and cheese, no bun and a side salad or a chicken Caesar salad without croutons. I don't regularly bake 'keto' desserts, but if I feel I need a little something I will have a little cream cheese with a few berries and whipped cream. It feels like I am having cheesecake without the guilt!

I find sticking with the basics, i.e. real food is so easy for me."[29]

The above testimonies have proved the effectiveness of the

---

[29] (Åkesson & Dr. Andreas Eenfeldt, 2019)

ketogenic diet. Although the ketogenic diet was originally developed to treat epilepsy, over the years, it has proven its versatility and its ability to evolve and treat other disorders and health issues most especially in the aspect of weight loss and keeping the body healthy and fit both mentally and physically.

Chapter Four: Why The Ketogenic Diet Works

Many people have emphasized the efficacy of the ketogenic diet and how it works wonders, but the main question that lies within is that how and why does the ketogenic diet work?

I would explain the secret behind the ketogenic diet. As it has been mentioned earlier in the previous sections, the ketogenic diet works through the process of being in a state called ketosis.

How can this state be reached? To reach the state of ketosis means that there is an absence of blood sugar in the body, which is glucose. But how can there be an absence of blood sugar since it is regarded as the fuel of the body? Can the body live without the presence of glucose? Yes, and yes, the body does well without the presence of glucose. Glucose is obtained after breaking down carbohydrate intake in the body.

This carbohydrate intake is stored in the body. Because the body can definitely not use all the intake You might be wondering and might be asking yourself, how did I gain weight? I did not consume junk like chocolates, sweets, ice cream, yet I am gaining weight? I have an answer to your questions.

You might be wondering after all has been emphasized on the effectiveness of the ketogenic diet, how does it really work and how can I be sure that it will solve my problems?

The ketogenic diet is a meal plan that consists of very low carbohydrate, minimal protein and very high in fats.

After the engagement of this diet, the body would be short on glucose, otherwise known as blood sugar, which is taken from carbohydrates. At this moment, there is nothing to "*fuel*" the body. The fat you consume, and the fat you stored previously, when broken down, will produce fatty acids and ketones.

These ketones would be transferred around the body and then transported to the brain. It assumes the work of glucose without issues. When it reaches a certain point in this engagement, the body's fuel supply is solely on ketones. This state is known as ketosis.

Ketosis is known for its efficacy in weight reduction and solving other disorders. During its inception, the ketogenic diet was and is still known for its effectiveness in treating epilepsy.

At this moment, there is nothing to "*fuel*" the body. The fat you consume, and the fat you stored previously, when broken down, will produce fatty acids and ketones.

These ketones would be transferred around the body and then transported to the brain. It assumes the work of glucose without issues. When it reaches a certain point in this engagement, the body's fuel supply is solely on ketones. This state is known as ketosis.

Ketosis is known for its efficacy in weight reduction and solving other disorders. During its inception, the ketogenic diet was and is still known for its effectiveness in treating epilepsy.

Misconceptions And Wrong Thoughts About Ketogenic Diet

The ketogenic is widely accepted by all and this is due to

its effectiveness. This has made a lot of people question its goodness and therefore developed a lot of misconceptions from it.

Some of these misconceptions are from people's ignorance, their fears and also the fact that keto can do the seemingly impossible, which makes it so hard for them to believe. Below are but a few misconceptions people have in regards to the ketogenic diet:

YOU CAN CONSUME AS MUCH FAT AS YOU WANT

Being on a keto diet does not give you the free rein to eat as much fat as you wish just to get your fats in. Although about 75% of your meal in a keto diet should be fat, that does not mean you can eat as many saturated fats as you so desire.

Unsaturated fats are actually the preferred and recommended option by dieticians and health professionals; it has also been confirmed by studies and research. IT IS REALLY DANGEROUS

There have been a lot of speculations that the ketogenic diet is very dangerous. This can happen to people who do not follow the ketogenic diet judiciously and to heart.

It has been said to cause a mineral deficiency, a high increase in cholesterol level and so on. It has also been said to cause heart disease. All these can be duly avoided if you hit and know your macros and micronutrients daily and you also ensure that you stay hydrated, and then all these downsides can be totally avoided and disarmed.

KETOSIS AND KETOACIDOSIS ARE TOTALLY THE SAME

The belief that ketosis and ketoacidosis are the same has been roaming all around but the two are totally different. "Ketosis is the metabolic process of using fat as the primary source of energy instead of carbohydrates. This means your body is directly breaking down its fat stores as energy instead of slowly converting fat and muscle cells into glucose for energy."[30]

That was according to Perfect Keto. Ketoacidosis, on the other hand, can be seen in diabetic patients who follow the ketogenic diet. Ketoacidosis is a "condition resulting from

---

[30] ("Ketosis Explained: What It Is, How to Achieve It (And Why You Want To)", n.d.)

dangerously high levels of ketones and blood sugar," according to Healthline. This causes the blood to become too acidic, and it affects organ function.

KETOGENIC DIET IS A HIGH PROTEIN DIET

The ketogenic diet is not a high protein diet. A ketogenic diet should consist of 75% fat, 20% protein, and 5% carbohydrate. If it were to be a high protein diet, it would have a protein percentage of between 30-35%.

FASTING IS A REQUIREMENT FOR KETO DIET

This is one I would like to really lay emphasis on. Fasting is not a requirement for ketogenic diet. It is not recommended to add fasting to your diet until you are already used to the system.

However, intermittent fasting alongside the ketogenic diet has its own benefits. It increases detoxification, weight loss and it also helps you reduce cravings and hunger. It should be well noted that you do not engage in intermittent fasting alongside your keto diet unless you have mastered the diet like reducing your carbohydrate intake level.

KETO DIET IS ALCOHOL RESISTANCE

Being in the ketogenic diet does not really mean alcohol should be totally avoided. Although most wines and alcohols are high carbohydrate sources, some alcohols are very low in carbohydrates, keto friendly like gin, vodka etc.

Alcohol should not be totally removed from the question but all is required of you is to be conscious of what you choose and be careful of how you drink while on the keto diet. It is important for you to note that your alcohol tolerability would be lower while you are on a ketogenic diet.

KETOGENIC DIET IS ONLY GOOD FOR WEIGHT LOSS

This is one of the persistent ketogenic diet myths and misconception. This belief connotes that the ketogenic diet is only and solely beneficial for people who are engaging in it for the purpose of weight loss. Do not be confused here, I did not say ketogenic diet is not useful for weight loss; it is a great and very effective tool for weight reduction but it can do a lot more.

Studies haves shown that the ketogenic diet promotes

weight loss and it also helps to counteract many vices that increase risk of heart disease and some metabolic symptoms. Not only this, but it has also proven to:

- Likely increase the lifespan

- To decrease food and sugar cravings

- To increase energy levels

- To increase mitochondrial health

- To ease inflammatory skin conditions

- Reduce the probability of having several chronic diseases like diabetes, chronic fatigue, cancer, neurodegeneration

- Cuts system inflammation

THE BRAIN NEEDS SUGAR TO FUNCTION

This misconception is really common amidst a great percentage of the world's population. The belief that the brain needs sugar to function and be able to perform effectively.

Thus, glucose is referred to as the fuel of the body. The illogical reasoning behind this is that glucose is taken from the carbohydrates we take in and the ketogenic diet promotes a drastic reduction in the intake of carbohydrates, so if the intake of carbohydrate which is the source of glucose reduces greatly, the body and brain will not function properly and effectively.

The ignorance in this is that the increase and decrease in fats and carbohydrates respectively are very beneficial to the body, and the fats, when broken down, produces ketone bodies which effectively replaces the glucose in the fuelling and effective functionality of the brain.

It carries out the work of the subsidized glucose and brings along added advantages like improvement in mental alertness, cognition. It has been shown by studies that the ketogenic diet has huge benefits in reducing the symptoms in Alzheimer's patients, and this is achieved by switching the brain to work on ketones instead of glucose.

Above are various examples of misconceptions regarding the ketogenic diet. The above have are facts against those misconceptions.

If you have any other questions regarding the ketogenic diet or you have concepts that seem misty or unclear, you should visit a dietician or a health professional.

This brings us to the end of the chapter, in light of the above segments; the meaning of ketogenic diet has been duly explained.

The history and development of the ketogenic diet have been explained as well.

You have learned that the ketogenic diet was originally invented for the treatment of epilepsy and seizures in little children but along the way, it was discovered that it does a lot more than the treatment of epilepsy.

The process behind the ketogenic diet has also been explained. How it works, what is required for this to happen? We have also laid emphasis on the various misconceptions of people regarding the ketogenic diet like the belief that you can eat as much fat as you want, and the misconception that the ketogenic diet is very dangerous. All these have been rebutted and well explained.

Chapter Five: Why You Should Engage In Ketogenic Diet And Intermittent Fasting For Weight Loss

I have received a lot of questions regarding the use of the ketogenic diet. Many people ask, why should I engage in this ketogenic diet? How is it better than other weight loss programs? Why should I fast to lose weight? Is it logical to do so? How does it work? Is it really effective?

Tom is a 61-year-old man who weighs 87 kg. When he was 59 years old, he was an obese man with high blood pressure, high cholesterol and so on. His doctors were thrilled that he reduced weight drastically and not only that, there was a significant change in his life.

People were wondering what gave him such drive, was it

because a friend of his died recently? Or was it because there was a reunion coming up? All these were true but are not the reason.

Tom has a daughter named Alina; she is 28 years old. She was working successfully as an accountant. She was happy and successful. Alina had occasional headaches but the doctors did not pay attention to it. In September 2016, she was rushed to the emergency room. The doctors found a massive tumor in her brain. She had two surgeries to remove the tumor. The news was that she was suffering from glioblastoma. It is an aggressive fast-growing brain cancer. The average survival for this was 12 months.

After the surgery, they decided to join a ketogenic diet study. It is not expected, right? Who prescribes that for a cancer treatment?

But this was not a random decision made; they found out through research that the ketogenic diet treats cancer. Now they could have gone through any other therapy and treatments. Tom, who was obese, could have done several other things but why ketogenic diet? Tom joined Alina as her coach and chef.

The ketogenic diet does not entirely cure cancer but the diet has shown promise for some cancers especially GBM. How is this so? On a simplistic level, cancer eats glucose and needs 20 times more glucose compared to other cells. Cancer cells cannot make the transition to using ketones, especially in the brain, making them more vulnerable to chemo and radiation.

The first two weeks for them was hard to start with. They gave up a lot of comfort foods. So, switching to a ketogenic diet is not the first thing that pops to your head when you hear cancer but the diet works. Tom steadily lost weight without substantial hunger or changes to his exercise program. His overall health improved drastically, he slept better and the change I mentioned earlier was that his daughter Alina, today, is a cancer survivor.

They are now two years behind her initial diagnosis and there has been no evidence of tumor regrowth. The ketogenic diet has really helped them overcome their challenges. Tom has lost 48 kg.

The evident reasoning here is that they could have done other therapies but the ketogenic diet came to their rescue.

The ketogenic diet and intermittent fasting are always easier means of weight reduction. I could remember the case of an obese boy who was bullied and mocked in school.

At all cost, he wanted to lose weight but whenever he went jogging, people would always make fun of him; if he went to the gym in his school, his mates bullied and it was kind of embarrassing for him because he was socially mocked and this affected him psychologically.

He was not mentally inclined any longer. He was introduced to the ketogenic diet and intermittent fasting; such a relief!

He was no longer laughed at while reducing weight because all he did was private. Nobody knew what he was eating, the number of carbohydrates he took in. And with time, he lost 30kg. He was no longer bullied and ridiculed.

If your story or situation is similar to the boy, it is never too late to begin. If you have been shamed and mocked for your situation, the ketogenic diet is here for you. It is not compulsory that people know you are going through a weight reduction scheme. You can also engage in intermittent fasting in the confines of your room and nobody would know about it.

Most people lose on their weight loss schemes due to many reasons. A friend of mine misses her gym class due to prolonged meetings until I made her know the efficacy of ketogenic diet and intermittent fasting. She does not have to leave meetings. Many of you are trying to lose weight but because of your busy schedule and work, you cannot easily accomplish your fitness goals. Why bother? The ketogenic diet is here for you.

Some of you have very busy and time-consuming professions, like bankers, accountants, engineers, doctors and so on. For example, a banker who has to be in front of a desk all day attending to customers has no time to schedule for his or her fitness and weight reduction schemes.

Why not go through the ketogenic diet and also fast intermittently? This will not hinder your job effectiveness or time schedule, but would rather boost your mental alertness, your cognitive development and would really increase your work efficiency.

Is that not a great and effortless offer? All you have to do is to take the step and discover a world of ease and great outcome.

Other Weight Loss Programs That You Can Replace With The Ketogenic Diet And Intermittent Fasting

There are weight loss programs that the ketogenic diet and intermittent fasting can substitute. This may be due to various reasons and influencing factors. Let us examine some of these below and try to understand why this is so.

Going to the gym

It is evident that whenever someone says that he or she wants to lose some weight, the first statement that family and friends would say is, "*why not hit the gym?*"

This is why you can get your desired body and you can work out your fitness goals. I would be laying down some sample cases and we would have to decide at the end of the day.

A woman that is unemployed goes to the gym to work out daily and reach her fitness goals. Fortunately for her, she got a job into a firm a company as their lawyer. So the woman will not be able to go to the gym again.

You might be wondering why this is so? She would have several cases and preparations, she would be so busy that there will not be time for her to hit the gym, and over time she gains weight.

Although she is making money, and this is good, there is a saying I love that says *"health is wealth."*

She is not able to take care of her health again. Sometimes if she comes back from work late at night, she would be so tired to cook and she would eat junk.

All this can be solved through the introduction of the ketogenic diet. She would not have to make time out of her busy schedule and eat junk again but still, she is losing weight.

Our second case is that of a movie producer. It is evident that movie producers have to spend most of their time on set and locations.

Such an individual will not be able to go to the gym and therefore his or her fitness goals are gradually ruined. Why not go into intermittent fasting: most directors don't have a problem with missing or skipping meals. There are various times they would have to shoot some scenes by 3am. They can continually shoot a scene throughout the morning and even forget they have not eaten. Is that not an opportunity? That is a means of turning a demerit into an added advantage. All you have to do is to draw out a plan but it is advisable to see a doctor before you commence in order to know if you can do it or not. The ketogenic diet has made weight loss very easy.

Use of herbal medicines and drugs

You might be wondering how the ketogenic diet and intermittent fasting would supplement or replace this. It would be such a great feeling of joy and happiness if you realize that a single drug can make you lose and shed weight.

The stress of going to the gym and so on would be uplifted. Even in our society today, such drugs are rampant. The government will do anything in its capacity to subsidize the price of such drugs because the result it brings is very enticing. It reduces the rate at which people develop heart diseases and this indirectly reduces the rate at which people die in society. But with that, some of them are still quite exorbitant in price. We are going to look at the case of a woman named Grace.

Grace is an accountant. She is very successful and quite diligent at everything she does. She is very resourceful. Grace went to learn culinary arts and cooking. She was the catch to all men's eyes.

But unfortunately for those men, she was in a relationship. But then her boyfriend broke up with her which really left Grace devastated. It was a relationship of 5 years. She cried for weeks. She had only one companion that kept her through those times: it was junk food.

After she got over the trauma of the heartbreak, she could not get over the way she now eats junk. She ate junk and could not stop it.

With time, she started gaining a lot of weight, her waistline increased massively. The once beautiful Grace, the aim of all men became just "*adorable*". This was brought to her friends' notice and they told her about a herbal drug that reduces the weight of its users.

She was very happy that she found a solution to her

problems at last. What a relief! She started taking the herbal pill but still, there was no improvement. Instead she still gained more and more weight. You might be wondering why this is so? The problem she has is not with her body but with her habit. The drug she was using was to make her a change in her body but the causative factors was still left untreated.

She was later introduced to the ketogenic diet and intermittent fasting. This totally worked because the problem she was having was not with her body but with her habit, and the ketogenic diet changes your habit and lifestyle because it is not just a diet, it is a lifestyle.

This also relates to most people who are solely dependent on drugs and see no improvement. The problem is not your body system, but your habitual trait which can only be corrected by a remedy that deals with a lifestyle approach and this is the ketogenic diet.

So what are you waiting for? It is never too late to start. I believe in the saying that goes thus, *"A journey of a thousand miles begins with a step."*

Jogging and other forms of exercise

This system of body fitness and weight reduction is mostly used by everybody but is it really everybody? Waking up in the morning, if you look outside your window, you would see a lot of people, most especially your neighbors, going for a jog.

You wish you could join them as before but why is this not so. We might have the same traits as human beings but we are quite peculiar in our different ways. As our fingerprints do not match with any other person's own, so are our traits.

You wish you could also lace up your shoes every morning and go out for a jog. Not everybody is inclined to that. Some of us cannot afford to go for a mile jog and still have to get to the office very early in the morning. We are going to look at three sample cases in our plot.

Abigail is a very athletic person in school. She has got the shape and the brains. She ran track in high school and is a very good jogger. She is always after her body fitness and how to stay healthy. Now she is married with two kids. After she had her first child, she resorted to going back into jogging and keeping fit until she realized she was already pregnant again.

She did not have time for herself again, she had to take care of the children, prepare breakfast early in the morning, and she lost the zeal for early morning jogging. She started gaining some extra weight because she was stress eating.

The problem she has now is that she has a college reunion coming up in 5 months and it would be so embarrassing if her mates see that the once ever fit Abigail is now an obese woman. What can she do?

Abraham is a banker. He is very fit and also a body trainer. On one of his meetings with a client, he had an accident. This was a very terrible accident. He almost lost his legs. He was no longer on wheelchairs but he cannot walk for a long time. This made him really down; he ate and consumed junk in all kinds and forms. He is becoming quite obese and his fiancée is about to break up with him unless he loses some weight. What can he do?

Richard is very reactive to how he looks and what he puts into his body; his friends call him a fitness freak. Richard lost it all when he lost his parents and siblings in a car crash. He was the only one that survived the crash. He lost one of his legs and he became frustrated. It was so bad that he tried committing suicide. He ate and ate. Now he has found redemption and love through a woman he refers to as his God-sent angel. He is now overweight. He wants to make a difference in his weight, but how can he do it?

To Abigail, I know being a mother is quite tiring and time-consuming but you have got to do all it takes. It is not really compulsory for you to jog before you can lose but have you not heard of the ketogenic diet? You do not have to jog again, just form a meal plan for your diet and start following it judiciously and I can assure you that before your college reunion you would be even fit than you used to be. So start the ketogenic diet today and you would see the difference.

To Abraham, I would advise you to not stress yourself too much since you are still recuperating. You need to see a doctor in order to know if you are fit to start the ketogenic diet because of your status. If you are approved to do so, it would be a wonderful experience because you would be amazed at the outcome. I would advise you not to add intermittent fasting alongside the ketogenic diet because of situations whereby you have to use drugs and supplements.

To Richard, I know you were hurting and you did not have control over your habits. I know for sure that you still have a purpose and it must be fulfilled. It is quite nice, the way you want to redeem yourself. It is a very simple thing because I have a remedy for you. The ketogenic diet is very effective in such cases. You have to be diligent and follow it strictly and I am sure you would have yourself redeemed and you will have no reason to feel depressed about life and its challenges.

It has been shown in our cases above that the ketogenic diet is very effective in replacing jogging for people with some peculiarities.

Employing the use of work-out videos

Not everybody is able to go to a gym and workout or meet their fitness goals. This may be due to various reasons. To some, it is the stress of having to go to the gym. And to some other people, it is the unavailability of time. To most other people, it is due to the fact that they do not want to be mocked by others in the gym or while jogging. So they resort to the use of workout DVD. Most people cannot afford to pay the fee to gym classes, so why not use an affordable DVD instead?

The workout DVD is very affordable and you can do it in the confines of your home. But is there a disadvantage to this? We are going to look at the stories of two or three people in order for us to understand better.

Leslie is a sales representative of a pharmaceutical company. She is uptight and all about her weight. She could not afford the fee to be a member of the gym so she bought a workout DVD and she started her fitness journey.

Very good news hit her and she was very delighted about this. She was being considered for a promotion at work. She began to work over her schedule in order to impress the management and be given the promotion. She gradually stopped having time for herself and her body. She added some pounds to her weight due to the fact that she did not have time to cook again, all she ate was junk. At times during the weekend, when she's tired, she treats herself to a late night snack of chicken and a bag of potato chips. She gained 15 pounds. When she realized the changes in her weight, she was petrified that she was going to lose the promotion. What is she to do?

Danny is a lawyer. He has three kids and a beautiful wife.

Few years into their marriage, he gained some weight and this was due to the stress of having to provide for the family and fend for the extended family. Due to his busy schedule, he could not apply to a gym but his wife bought him a workout DVD to use. This was great news to him. He started using the workout DVD and it was effective. He was then offered to be a partner, but it was still months away. He started doing everything in his power to make sure he got the partnership because he had competitors. He had totally forgotten about the workout DVD and started gaining more weight. This was to his surprise; he did not want his wife to come back and meet him obese, because she traveled. He was left in a confusing state, the reason being that if his wife came back and met him obese she would not take it lightly with him and if he starts working out, he will not have time to chase his lifetime opportunity of being a partner. What will he do?

Hillary is a very successful woman. She has three kids and a loving husband. Unfortunately, her husband died in an accident. She was left all alone with three kids; she was very depressed and stressed out. She had to take care of the children and also fend for herself. She gained a lot of weight. On realizing this, she went to register at a gym but on hearing the time schedule, she could not make it. So, she bought a workout DVD and started the fitness program but along the line, she could not carry on due to the responsibilities on her alone. She gained more and more weight. She is wondering about the way out for her. What will she do?

To all three sides, this is a very compromising condition. For the case of Leslie, as I have said earlier, health is wealth. Do not deprive yourself of good health all because you want wealth.

I have a solution to your worries. You do not have to worry or give yourself unnecessary stress because the ketogenic diet is here to help. The problem is the unavailability of time, so you need a measure that does not take valuable time away from you. You can be on the ketogenic diet and still have enough time for your promotion goals to work out. All you have to do is to control your carbohydrate intake, minimize the amount of protein you take in and increase your fat intake. I can assure you of a positive outcome and a well-fitted body to take up that promotion.

To Danny, life is full of various solutions; you just have to explore it. I would proffer a solution that is well tested and trusted to you. The ketogenic diet, started today, and your wife would meet a completely different man compared to what she left and you would be surprised yourself.

To Hillary, I know life might be hard sometimes but do not let it bring you down or diminish who you are. Try the ketogenic diet today and you would see the difference.

I know that these cases might relate to you in one way or the other. The ketogenic diet is here for you. Not alone will it fight your weight problems but also treat other disorders in your body.

Chapter Six: Benefits Of Intermittent Fasting

In the world of health and health management, intermittent fasting is coming back to fame and popular recognition. The history of intermittent fasting could be traced back to the dawn of man. It has been a great advantage to man. Below are some of the benefits of intermittent fasting:

1. It improves fat burning

2. It increases weight and body fat loss

3. It increases your energy level

4. It lowers sugar levels and blood insulin

5. It improves mental clarity and concentration

6. It reverses type 2 diabetes

7. It increases the growth hormone

8. It lowers the blood cholesterol level

9. It potentially elongates the lifespan

10. It reduces inflammation.

1. IMPROVES FAT BURNING

This is one of the main benefits of intermittent fasting. It rapidly increases the rate at which fats in the body burns. The schedule of your fasting burns fats. The fats in your body are caused by excess carbohydrates that are stored up. So, not eating at intervals will reduce the rate at which you eat, and this will reduce your fat level.

2. IT INCREASES WEIGHT AND BODY FAT LOSS

The intermittent fasting weight loss programs have been known for effectiveness in the rapid loss of weight by its users, and it also reduces body fat. It is trending now because of its outcome and various testimonies people have made. It reduces the rate at which you eat, therefore reducing your body weight and fat.

3. IT INCREASES YOUR ENERGY LEVEL

You might be wondering how fasting which is quite tiring to you makes you get energy. The main reason for being overweight is because of the unused carbohydrate that has been stored up. So being on an intermittent fasting schedule would definitely reduce the fat and the rest would be fully which will promote a faster generation of energy. Furthermore, if the body is enlightened from the excess fat in it, it will be able to carry out more functions. Also, as the saying goes, "*A healthy body is an agile body.*"

4. IT LOWERS SUGAR LEVELS AND BLOOD INSULIN

Studies have shown that intermittent fasting reduces the level of blood sugar in the body. Intermittent fasting as a process in which the level of eating is limited during certain times of the week helps men and women to lose a massive amount of weight and also helps in reducing their insulin. Oftentimes, diabetes is treated as a drug-related condition not with therapies and diet, and treating it with drugs never addresses the root of the problem of diabetes. Weight has been said to help people reduce insulin resistance and it also helps to absorb blood sugar more effectively.

5. IT IMPROVES MENTAL CLARITY AND CONCENTRATION

This is a crucial benefit that intermittent fasting brings to man. The shedding of excess weight and fat makes the cognitive development increase rapidly. Let us look at a story of Tony. Tony is a high school kid but he is obese and he was always mocked and bullied by his mates. He was introduced to intermittent fasting by one of his mother's friends. After weeks of the therapy, his life changed. His self-confidence increased and his attention to his studies also. His fears were alleviated and he began to excel in class. He was mentally alert.

It has been proven that intermittent fasting increases the rate at which we think. Some experts have explained that most obese patients have issues with depression and tend to always feel down about themselves, but on losing weight, those fears and depression will be uplifted and this brings about more alertness mentally.

In most cases, this is mostly not true, the reason being that the reduction in the way we eat also helps our brain increase its functionality and thereby promoting alertness and sharpness in the person.

6. IT REVERSES TYPE TWO DIABETES

It is a great advantage to the world that intermittent fasting reverses this condition. Type 2 diabetes is caused by the body's resistance to insulin and increased blood sugar.

These are some of the benefits derived while doing intermittent fasting. It reduces the blood cholesterol level. It also elongates the lifespan through the treatment of blood sugar level, blood cholesterol level, and it has also been known to treat Alzheimer's disease and other syndromes.

The benefits of intermittent fasting take a long and large catalog and cannot be mentioned in words but rather through experience. So, why not start today and see its various benefits.

Benefits Of The Ketogenic Diet

The benefits of the ketogenic diet have a large catalog. The ketogenic diet provides a long range of benefits and treatments. When it was invented, the sole purpose was to cure and treat seizures in little children. The ketogenic diet came into limelight when testimony was shared by Charlie Abrahams. Research and studies have shown that the ketogenic diet rapidly reduces the weight of the patient.

Below are but a few benefits of the ketogenic diet:

1] The ketogenic diet has its efficacy in the reduction of

weight and body fat. The reduction of weight and body fat in the body while engaging in the ketogenic diet is through the state of ketosis. Ketosis has been known to drastically reduce body weight because, during this state, the body fats that have been stored up will be burned up and be used, thereby causing a large reduction of weight in the body of such individual. To get into this state of ketosis is not quite easy but it can be achieved through the ketogenic diet. The ketogenic diet increases fat intake, and when they are broken down, will bring out ketones that serve this purpose.

2] The ketogenic diet increases the mental agility and alertness of its patients. This has been proved by various people that have benefitted from the ketogenic diet. As explained in the previous chapter, the ketogenic diet reduces depression in its patients which makes them more active. By the mere absence of the blood sugar, the ketogenic diet helps the functionality of the brain which makes the brain function better and increases the cognitive prowess of such an individual.

3] The ketogenic aids the control of the blood sugar level. The ketogenic diet aids the reduction and the perfect control of blood sugar level. The meal structure of the ketogenic diet tells it all. The sugar in the blood is caused by the excess intake of carbohydrates and the ketogenic diet curbs this by making a meal plan that reduces the intake of carbohydrates we take in and increases the number of fats.

4] The ketogenic diet has mastery in the treatment of seizures in epileptic patients, especially small children. Tracing the history of the ketogenic diet, it can be found that the ketogenic diet was originally designed to treat seizures and reduce the chances in little children. This has been a great help to the human race at the same time. Even when the anticonvulsant drugs fail, medical practitioners resort to the ketogenic diet for help.

5] The ketogenic diet also treats disorders and diseases like the Alzheimer's disease, heart disease, fatty liver, and numerous diseases.

6] The ketogenic diet has been proven to elongate and increase one's lifespan. This might be surprising to you but studies have shown that this is certified and authentic. The alleviation and reduction in weight and body fat reduce the rate at which one becomes a victim of life-taking diseases. The ketogenic diet through its effective treatment of seizures in epileptic patients and this has been known to reduce the rate at which the disease becomes deadly.

In light of the above, the benefits that the ketogenic diet brings to its patients are quite convincing that it is the perfect diet for you. So, why not try it out today and you would see that your life will never remain the same!

Chapter Seven: Different Types And Kinds Of Intermittent Fasting

The intermittent fasting varies in types and has many diverse ways of doing and engaging in it. Below are some different ways to go about intermittent fasting:

1] The 16/8 method: This is fasting for 16 hours each day. This method as I have said earlier involves the fasting for 14-16 hours and solely restricts your eating window to 8-10 hours each day.

With this, one is permitted to eat around 2-3 meals. This method of fasting is also known as the Leangains protocol and this was propounded and popularized by fitness expert Martin Berkhan. This method is as easy as not eating anything for dinner or skipping breakfast.

For example, if you eat dinner around 8 pm, all you have to do is to not eat anything until 12 noon the following the day. This makes you technically fasted for 16 hours. It is advised that women should only fast 14-15 hours because they do much better with slightly shorter fasts.

This might be really hard and not easy to adhere to by people who are fond of eating in the morning or having late night snacks. It will be very comfortable for people who skip breakfast because that is essentially how they eat.

If you are not quite comfortable with the early morning hunger, you can take water, coffee, and other beverages. They also serve as a means of reducing hunger levels and the temptation of sneaking in a snack for you.

You should note that it is of utmost importance to eat very healthy foods during your window period. The fact that you are engaging in intermittent fasting does not warrant you to eat excess junk. Consuming a lot of calories during your window period is likely to hinder the effects of the intermittent fasting.

Personally, I find this to be the most natural way of fasting because I also do it. It has been proven that late night snacks are not extensively digested by our digestive system, thereby causing a redundant amount of excess fats and calories not burned in our body.

This is also effortless; not only are you doing your digestive system a favor, but you are also benefiting from it in several other ways. Let me use myself as an example, I also engage in the ketogenic diet, so I am really not hungry until around 1 pm in the afternoon. Later on, I eat my last meal around 6-9pm. With this, I end up fasting for 16-19 hours each day.

The summary and bottom line of this is that the 16/8 method consists of daily fasting of 16 hours for men and advisably 14-15 hours for women. This leaves you with an 8-hour window of eating which will range 2-3 meals.

It is highly advisable not to take advantage of this window and eat excess junk or take in too many calories. This will hinder the effectiveness of the fasting and results may not be as you expected.

2] The 5:2 diet: this means that you will fast for 2 days a week. This involves you eating normally for 5 days and then fasting for the remaining 2 days whereby you restrict your intake of calories between the ranges of 500-600.

This is also known as the fast diet. It was popularized by a renowned doctor and a British journalist Michael Mosley. It is advisable that women eat 500 calories and men eat 600 calories on these fasting days.

For example, you might decide that the two days you want to fast are on Mondays and Wednesdays. So it is expected that on these days you eat two meals each consisting 250 calories for women and each consisting 300 calories for men. As critics rightly pointed out, there is no valid study testing this diet but there are many studies and research that have tested and proven the intermittent fasting to be effective and very useful in the reduction of weight and other benefits. So we can rightly say since this diet is a form of intermittent fasting, it can be said to be effective and reliable.

The bottom line of what is above is that the intermittent fasting involves eating 500 calories for women and 600 calories for men for two days of the week but they can freely eat normally for the other 5 days that are left.

3] Eat-Stop-Eat: It means the fasting is done for 24 hours. This approach to intermittent fasting involves the fasting for 24 hours once or twice a week. This method was popularized by the renowned fitness expert Brad Pilon and this method has been in trend for quite some years now.

If you fast from dinner today to dinner tomorrow, it means you have fasted for 24 hours. For example, if you finish eating dinner by 8 pm on Friday and you do not eat until 8 pm on Saturday, it means that you have fasted for 24 hours straight. The option used in the 16/8 diet can also be used due to the longevity in the fast. Non-caloric beverages like coffee, water and so on can be taken during the fast but no solid food is allowed during the fast. The reason is that those beverages have been known to be a very useful tool in reducing hunger level. Therefore, they reduce the rate of temptations to break the fast.

If you are doing this to lose weight, it is very important to note that, it is very crucial to eat normally during your window period. The fact that you just fasted for 24 hours does not warrant you to eat excessively on your non-fasting days. So, the amount of food should be minimized.

One of the biggest problems of this form of intermittent fasting is that it is very difficult to follow since it is for a full 24 hours. You might be wondering how you would go into it right away. It is not compulsory to start straight away, you can start with 14-16 hours and then you can move upward from there. I can testify to this, I have done it a few times.

The beginning would be very easy but the ending hours will be like hell. That is why I went to the 14-16 hours and now it has increased to 16-19 hours. So, it is not really something that you start up straight away.

In a few words, the Eat-Stop-Eat method of intermittent fasting involves a fasting routine which entails 24 hours fast for one or two days each week.

4] Alternate Day fasting: The alternate day fasting means that you fast every other day. There are many versions of this method. Most of them allow about 500 calories when you are on your fasting days. Various labs studies that show the benefits of intermittent fasting used some versions of this method. A full fast every other day seems too extreme, so I really do not recommend this for beginners.

Going through this method, you will be going to your bed hungry many times each week. This is not really pleasant and it is quite unsustainable on a long-term basis.

The Alternate day fasting simply means that you are fasting every other day, it can be by not eating anything at all or by eating a few hundred calories.

5] The Warrior diet: This name might sound absurd for a diet but it means fasting during the day and eating a huge meal at night. This diet method was popularized by a fitness expert named Ori Hofmekler. This diet involves you eating a small or minimal amount of vegetables and fruits during the day and eating one huge meal at night. This basically means that you fast all day and you feast at night within a 4-hour window.

This diet was one of the popular diets to include the intermittent fasting. This diet has also been said to embrace food choices that are closely related to the paleo diet. From my point of view, this diet has a history which has been depicted by the name. Warrior diet can be similarly traced to the ancient times when the warriors would leave for battlefield early in the morning. They would only eat a few things they can find on the way like fruits and vegetables. After the battle, they would return at night and, merry, feast like kings. They would eat a lot and sleep. The cycle begins the next day all over.

In essence, the warrior diet is all about eating little amounts of fruits and vegetables during the day and eating a huge meal in the night within a 4-hour eating window.

6] Spontaneous meal skipping: This simply means that you skip meals when it is convenient. This means that you do not have to follow a structured fasting plan, all you have to do is to skip meals when it is convenient for you. You can skip meals from time to time when you are probably too busy or you just do not feel like eating.

There is a myth that tells that humans have to eat from time to time or they will lose their muscle and reach starvation mode. As you might have well understood now, the human body is well structured and equipped to handle extended periods of famine, not to talk about missing one or two meals from time to time. It is quite easy to do, if you are not hungry, you can skip breakfast, or if you are in heavy traffic, instead of buying roadside snacks, why not do a short fast.

Not eating one or two meals is what spontaneous

intermittent fasting implies. Make sure you eat healthy foods during meals.

To cap it all, spontaneous fasting is the most natural way to do intermittent fasting and this is just by skipping one or two meals when you do not feel like eating or when you do not even have time to eat.

We have been able to examine various methods and approach to intermittent fasting. The question now is, how do I know the one that I will do? Just choose the one that is most convenient for you or you can seek the help of a dietician, a health professional and so on. Choose and start one today and you would never be the same!

Different Types Of The Ketogenic Diet

The ketogenic diet varies in types; there are various approaches by which someone can do the ketogenic diet and reach a state of ketosis. There are many types of ketogenic diets and each one of them is useful for different purposes.

You will compare each of them and then decide the path that you will take in order to reach your fitness goals. I will be sharing some of these approaches and types ketogenic diet to you. Below are the approaches and types of ketogenic diet:

1] The Standard ketogenic diet [SKD]: The standard ketogenic diet is the most basic form of the ketogenic diet. The goal of the SKD is to have 50 grams or less of carbohydrates each day in order to keep you in a state of ketosis. Your calories will be obtained from fats and proteins. This is actually the best place to get started with your diet and due to its effectiveness many people who have tested it have no reason to change to another type because of the positive results they got.

2] The Targeted ketogenic diet [TKD]: The aim of the Targeted ketogenic diet is to have you consume your carbohydrates during your workout times. It can be immediately before or immediately after your workout time.

This plan of diet is most useful to people that do workouts and exercise regularly. It can be the new athletes or it can be the ones that are highly trained. The carbohydrates should be kept very low, even though the workouts can increase carbohydrate tolerance. It is mostly done by people by consuming 30-50 grams of carbohydrate in order to maintain their energy levels during a workout.

3] The Cyclic ketogenic diet [CKD]: The cyclic ketogenic diet is mainly for advanced athletes that need a greater boost in carbohydrates for fuel during their training. These types of athletes include power lifters, endurance runners and professional players. They would consume a high level of carbohydrate for two days before their competition in order to fully reload their glycogen storage. This will really help them in their muscle growth and also their power, although it can also lead to fat storage.

4] The High protein ketogenic diet: This model of the ketogenic diet is mainly for the people that want to shed excess body fat. In the high protein ketogenic diet, the aim is to drop excess fat not just body weight from the body in general.

Through having a higher proportion of protein compared to fats, the body would be able to keep a lean muscle mass and to build muscle in the case of working out. To also make sure to use the fat that is already stored up in the body as fuel and this is even faster than the normal ketogenic diet. On this model, you would consume up to 1.5 grams of protein per pound of lean mass. This increase in protein to burn fats faster and makes it easier to lose fat while maintaining and gaining strength.

5] The Protein Sparing Modified Fast [PSMF]: This is a highly restrictive modification of the ketogenic diet. It includes mainly lean proteins and it is kept to 600-1000 calories a day. It is designed as a temporary solution to kick-start weight loss while preserving the muscle mass. Those that are on it avoid meat that is essentially higher in fat. Do not add fat while cooking and continue to avoid carbohydrates. The fat that produces the ketone bodies comes mainly from the fats that are stored up in the body. This model is a great temporarily; it is not sustainable as a lifestyle to its users.

Chapter Eight: Choosing The Perfect Intermittent Fasting For You

In light of the chapters before, you have seen various types of intermittent fasting and several approaches to them. It has been observed by psychologists that one of the uncertainties that reside in man are the inability to know the journey or challenge for him to engage in.

This is really hard, I know because there are various options to pick or select from and this is quite confusing. That is why I am here to help you go through this and achieve your prospective fitness goals.

As I have mentioned in the previous chapter, the intermittent fasting varies in methods and styles by which people approach it. I made mention of these methods, which include:

1] 16/8 method of fasting: This involves you fasting for

14-16 hours a day.

2] 5:2 diets: This involves fasting for 2 days a week.

3] Eat-Stop-Eat: This involves you fasting 24 hours for one or two days per week.

4] Alternate day fasting: This involves you fasting for every other day.

5] Warrior diet: This is an approach that can literally be likened to a warrior; it involves eating of fruits and vegetable throughout the day and eating a huge meal at night.

6] Spontaneous method: This happens to each and every one of us. It simply means skipping meals intentionally and occasionally when you are not really hungry or you are quite busy at work and other things. This is one of the most natural ways of carrying out the intermittent fasting.

There are various reasons that push people into carrying out the intermittent fasting. Some do it to shed weight, some to stay healthy; others do it to keep fit. There is a twist in this decision making, how would you know the perfect one for you? Let us look at a case.

Rebecca is a sales rep. She was quite surprised when she got on the scale and realized that she weighs 176 pounds. She was terrified and confused about how it happened. She went online and read some articles and books on losing weight. Then she saw an article about the intermittent fasting and its numerous advantages. She decided to do it. She also decides to be on the warrior diet because it looked promising and she thought it would yield a faster result that would help her to reach her fitness goals.

On the first day of her fast, the first hours were quite easy, she felt happy. But due to the nature of her job, she needed the energy to keep on. She started fading out and losing balance by 3 pm. Oh no, she must get something to eat. She rushed down to the nearest place she could get food and she ate. So sad, she could not keep up the fast. She was confused on what to do next since she has failed at the warrior diet. She was advised by a friend and co-worker of hers that it is advisable for her to go see a dietician in order to know which one suits her. She later went to the dietician and she was told that she has to start little by little.

The intermittent fasting process can be likened to the experience of a little boy and a bicycle. The boy had to go to the places he wanted to go like visiting friends on his foot. This was quite tiring to him. Then, he got a bicycle; this to him was the end of all his troubles. He decided to take his bicycle out one day and while going, he fell.

This was discouraging to him; he decided not to ride the bicycle ever again. Little did he know that to ride it is not easy? You will fall down a lot of times and by the time you get it, doing it will be very easy. You even close your eyes while riding it, and then you develop a lot of skills.

The intermittent fasting is not an easy scheme at first but this is due to your naivety to the scheme. After you finish learning about the skills, you will become an expert and could even teach other people encouraging them to never give up. To learn a bicycle would make you fall a lot of times but that is why I am here. To guide you through your challenge in order not to fall because most times, such falls could be very dangerous.

As a beginner in this program, try not to outdo yourself. Remember that you are new to the system, so is your body. Start little by little. It is most advisable to start with the 16/8 method or the spontaneous method. You could even form your own schedule. For example, let us say I am a accounts officer. This means I have to leave early in the morning. I could take a cup of coffee in the morning before going to work. Take some fruits and vegetables along in order to keep me sustained. When I get back in the evening, I will eat and this window would stop by 8-9 pm. The cycle continues. I can also decide to not take anything at all except water until I get back and eat my dinner. All depends on your schedule, work and most importantly your body. It is advisable to see a doctor before you start. This will let you know if you are fit to go or not. You should not disobey or disregard whatever the doctor says because if you do, it is highly detrimental to your health and life.

After some weeks, you will see that it is an easy thing to do because by then, you have gotten used to the system and you can now increase the hours by which you fast or change your approach to it in order to get more desired results.

Why not start today and see the goodness in intermittent fasting. Do not rush yourself all because you want to get a quick result. Take it slowly, as the saying goes, "*The journey of a thousand miles begins with a step."*

Choosing The Perfect Ketogenic Diet

The thought of having to make a choice most times puts most of us under pressure. I know it must be quite a task to choose the form of ketogenic diet you will do because of you want results and you would not want to partake in a type that does not bring out the desired result that you want. That is why I am here to guide you through and help you in choosing the perfect ketogenic diet. As I have mentioned earlier, the ketogenic diet has several approaches which include:

1] The Standard Ketogenic diet

2] The Targeted ketogenic diet

3] The Cyclic ketogenic diet

4] The High Protein ketogenic diet

5] The Protein Sparing Modified Fast

I am going to be explaining what each of them entails, the requirements, the rules and the type of people that it is most suitable for.

THE STANDARD KETOGENIC DIET

This is probably the most basic form of the ketogenic diet. It is used by most people who engage in the ketogenic diet. It entails the taking in of 50 grams of carbohydrate or less. This intake helps you to stay in the state of ketosis and it has been tested and trusted with the testimonies of people backing it up. The standard ketogenic diet is mostly used by the people who are new to the diet. It is meant for rapid weight loss, it is for people who desire to keep fit and lose weight. So, if you are almost obese or you are feeling that you have gained excess weight of recent. This is the best for you. It is quite easy; your energy supply would be coming from the proteins and fats that you eat. What it requires is just a drastic reduction in the of calories and carbohydrates you take in. It requires you to increase the number of fats you eat: this will supplement the energy supply that is being brought by carbohydrates.

If you are an office worker, this is the best for you. It works without stress.

THE TARGETED KETOGENIC DIET

If you love working out or exercising, then I think you might want to see this. The targeted ketogenic diet gives way for you to consume 30-50 grams of carbohydrates in a day. You might be wondering how you would burn the calories. It is quite simple. The TKD is mainly for people who work out and exercise, so the calories are burned during the workouts. The intake of the carbohydrate can be immediately before your workout or immediately after your workout. Calories are burn during workouts and exercise.

If you do not like to work out or exercise, this is really not for you. It can be that you are too busy to work out or go to the gym; this is not for you either. So, if your job is time-consuming, you are not advised to take on this approach to ketosis. If you have time on your schedule to spare, then this is designed for you.

There was a story of a woman. She exercises a lot but after her marriage, she lost it. She gained a lot of weight and could not keep fit again. She was about to go out to look for a job but she is afraid that she might not be accepted because of her body size. I would recommend this to her because not only will she lose weight and get a job but she would also be able to go back to her former hobby of exercising which has been said to keep the doctor away. So, to my exercise lovers: this is for you.

THE CYCLIC KETOGENIC DIET

As you already know, the ketogenic diet is not only known for the reduction of weight. It also treats other disorders like high blood pressure, heart disease, cancer, fatty liver and so on. This form of ketogenic diet is solely for athletes.

It is for professional athletes whose sports require a lot of energy like weight lifters, endurance runners, footballers and so on. If you are not one of these, it is not for you.

So, do not try it, else you would not see the desired results. The cyclic ketogenic diet requires a high level of carbohydrate consumption but these carbohydrates are later burned up during their sports activities. They would consume a high level of carbohydrate for two days before their competition in order to fully reload their glycogen storage. This will really help them in their muscle growth and also their power, although it can also lead to fat storage. This will really help in mental alertness, cognitive development and as said above improvement in muscle growth and power.

This is mainly for higher athletes. If you are not one: do

not try it because if you do, you will not be able to burn up such amount of carbohydrate and therefore instead of losing weight, you are actually gaining more weight.

THE HIGH PROTEIN KETOGENIC DIET

This approach to ketogenic diet is for people that want to shed excess fats. That is, if you are overweight or obese, this is the perfect diet for you. The aim of this diet is to remove excess fat from the body and the removal of excess fat storage. This requires a high protein diet and through this high protein the excess fats are shed and it keeps the muscle mass lean. It builds the muscle mass in case you want to work out and it also sheds the excess fat that is already stored in the body. What is surprising is that it does not only shed the excess fats in the body but also uses it as a means of energy. While doing this, you will have to consume 1.5 grams of protein per muscle mass. This form of diet helps you to burn fats faster. While losing fats, it maintains your strength and energy levels.

This diet is for people who want a fast result in order to reach their fitness goals. It is more like the standard ketogenic diet; it is just that the proteins are higher.

So, if you are obese, it is advisable you try this out and you will see the difference.

THE PROTEIN SPARING MODIFIED FAST

This is a highly restrictive modification of the ketogenic diet. It includes mainly lean proteins and it is kept to 600-1000 calories a day. It is designed as a temporary solution to kick-start weight loss while preserving the muscle mass. Those that are on it avoid meat that is essentially higher in fat. Do not add fat while cooking and continue to avoid carbohydrate. The fat that produces the ketone bodies comes mainly from the fats that are stored up in the body. This model is a great temporarily; it is not sustainable to go as a lifestyle to its users.

This diet is quite promising in light of people who are really overweight. The diet serves as a kind of head start into the weight reduction scheme. But it is not really advisable to go for a long-term kind of lifestyle.

Above are various approaches to the ketogenic diet. There are various requirements and instructions to follow. All you have to do is to imagine yourself in each of the approaches and see which of them fits your best wishes regarding your fitness goals. Also look out for the one that suits your schedule and work the most. It is best advised to see a doctor or a dietician in order to avoid repercussions regarding your health and well being. All have been laid down for you, choose one today and your life will never remain the same.

Chapter Nine: What To Eat And Not To Eat

It should not be a surprise to you seeing people who took the ketogenic diet but there was still no improvement, or after there was an improvement, they went back to their former self.

Do not be surprised because the reason for that is their ignorance or their unwillingness to follow the instructions on what to eat and what not to eat.

There have been many speculations going all around the internet that one does not need to follow any rules; you are free to do anything as long as you are doing the ketogenic diet. This is a blatant lie and unconfirmed rumor. Some of these were treated when we were talking about the various misconceptions regarding the ketogenic diet.

The feeling of freedom comes to mind when you start to see the wonderful effects of the ketogenic diet but these actions we carry out during or after the program affects the results we will see and this can be discouraging.

I am here to tell you the things you should do and things that you should not do at all during your ketogenic diet challenge.

WATCH THE FATS YOU EAT

This is one of the things you need to watch out for during your ketogenic diet challenge. You must extensively watch the type of fats you put in your system. Since the fats entail 80% of your meals, is it not worth watching?

DRINK A LOT OF WATER

It is advised by doctors and health professionals that staying hydrated during the diet helps in your weight reduction goals. Staying hydrated is key in achieving your fitness goals.

ALCOHOL INTAKE

The matter of alcohol intake has been a controversial one by many scholars and professionals. It has been said that alcohol should not be taken during the ketogenic diet. This is due to the carbohydrate concentration in most of the wines and beers, but not all. Some types of alcohol are actually carbohydrate free and that means that they are keto friendly. What should be watched is the way you consume it. Although, it has been shown that the ketogenic diet increases the resistance one has to alcohol.

JUNK AND LATE NIGHT SNACK

This is one of the things that you should step away from. I know that it is quite hard to keep away from these things because when we were lonely and no one was there for us, they kept us comfortable and feeling wanted.

But these things are what led to you to start doing the ketogenic diet. Most of the time you look into the mirror, you do not like what you see due to your excess weight and these are the things that caused the excess fat.

So, indirectly, you hate them, you just do not know it yet. This junk food is detrimental to your health and can debar you from reaching your fitness goals.

On the long run, they cause diabetes, high blood sugar level, kidney problems, liver diseases, and most of all, obesity, and this is what you are trying to prevent.

So eating junk is likened to you shooting yourself in the leg. The issue of midnight snacks is common to most of us. Sometimes, we just want to treat ourselves to a late night snack of chicken, potato chips, ice cream, chocolates, burger, and pizza and so on. This can be due to a hard day's work or you doing something spectacular and you decided to appreciate yourself. This is really bad and it affects your body system. You might be wondering how. Let me explain to you.

The body system has a time it is active and has time to rest. It has been said that the digestive system rests from 10pm-4am. So taking a midnight snack is not only taking the risk of indigestion but also wearing out your body organs because they have no time to rest. It can be tempting and will not be easy to drop, but look at it as a stumbling block to achieving your fitness goals. It is not an advice but a must that you stop late night snacking and eating junk. Abiding by this will hasten the rate at which you lose weight.

THINGS TO DO AND THINGS NOT TO DO
DO EXERCISE WHEN OPPORTUNE

If you are the exercising type, it is fully advised to exercise alongside your ketogenic diet challenge. There is a misconception that the ketogenic diet disallows the use of workouts during it. This is a blatant lie. The use of exercise while dieting helps in the restoration of your muscle mass, energy, and keeping fit.

In case your schedule does not allow you to go to the gym or exercise, it is not necessarily important to get into the gym. If you cannot get into the gym, you can also buy workout DVD that you can use in your house.

DO WATCH YOUR CALORIES

This is very important to the successful completion of your ketogenic diet challenge. Try to watch the number of calories that you take in because too much of it will not only ruin your results but also store up in your body system, which will lead you to gain more weight instead of losing it. So watch your calorie intake in order to get the desired result.

DO AVOID FAST FOOD

For the fact that you can easily get burgers in a fast food restaurant is not really healthy. The foods are filled with chemicals and preservatives. Most of the time, they do not use cheese that is real. Even the salad might have hidden sugar sometimes.

DO not search for information about something after you might have finished eating it. Search for the information before you start eating it.

Chapter Ten: Tips On Ketogenic Diet

I will be giving you some tips that will help you with your ketogenic diet challenge. The tips are kind of shortcuts to having a successful ketogenic diet.

CLEAR CARBOHYDRATES FROM YOUR KITCHEN

Most people will only stick to the ketogenic diet if they had access to healthy ketogenic foods. This will help you a lot in avoiding falling prey to the carbohydrate concentrated foods in your cabinet. Clean your kitchen from high-carbohydrate foods like pastry, bread, potatoes, soda, rice, and candy. This will help a long way in achieving the ketogenic diet.

HAVE KETOGENIC SNACKS AT HAND

Having to prepare a lot of homemade meals is a big challenge for people as regards the ketogenic diet. There is a solution for you: why not have ketogenic snacks instead whenever you are hungry and you are not at home?

You can buy ketogenic snacks like hard boiled eggs, beef jerky, pre-cooked bacon, pre-made guacamole and so on or you can have them on the go. You can prepare a lot of them and this will not allow you to buy carbohydrate-heavy snacks.

BUY A FOOD SCALE

This might sound surprising but it is quite crucial. As it has been said, "*Drops of water make an ocean.*" The amount of food you eat matters even to the tiniest form. Buy a food scale to measure your food and make sure you are eating the appropriate size because even the least can make a difference.

For example, 2 extra tablespoons of almond butter turn out to be an additional 200 calories and 6 grams of carbohydrates. It is not necessary you use the food scale till the end of your challenge. It is just for you to get the appropriate measurement then you can eyeball to measure it as you continue.

EXERCISE FREQUENTLY

I have mentioned a lot. Exercising allows your body to break down the glycogen it has in store. It also helps you to get fit and healthy. It also helps you in maintaining your muscle mass and strengthens you.

TRY INTERMITTENT FASTING

This is one of the most effective tips that can get you right on track to achieving your fitness goals. It helps you get into ketosis and lose weight. This means that you do not eat anything that contains calories for a given period of time. A study in Harvard has made it known that intermittent fasting manipulates your mitochondria in a way that the ketogenic diet also does and this elongates your lifespan. When you stop taking calories for some time, your body will start breaking down the excess glucose in your body obtained from consuming carbohydrates.

INCLUDE COCONUT OIL INTO YOUR DIET

Coconut oil contains fats called medium chain triglycerides which help you to quickly get into ketosis. Unlike other fats, the MCTs get quickly absorbed into the liver where they can be used for energy or they can be converted into ketones.

Frequently Asked Questions And Answers To Them

I will be answering frequently asked questions regarding

the ketogenic diet.

Can pregnant women do the ketogenic diet?

The ketogenic has appeared safe due to the women that have done it and the doctors that have administered it to their patients during pregnancy. I cannot say I am right because there is no scientific research or study that has proved this. So, there is a lack of knowledge concerning this. The ketogenic diet may be very helpful in case of gestational diabetes. It is therefore advised that caution is to be exercised for a ketogenic diet during pregnancy unless there is a benefit you want to achieve while doing it in your own case.

At what level should my ketones be during ketosis?

Your ketones should be above 0.5mmol/l and this is general.

Can I develop muscles while doing my ketogenic diet?

Sure! It is even advised to do so but it is not compulsory. You can do this by going to the gym to work out; you can even buy the workout DVD if you do not have the time to go to the gym. Like I said earlier, it is not compulsory.

How long can I be on the ketogenic diet?

As long as you want! That is why the ketogenic diet is often referred to as a lifestyle. You can do it as long as you desire.

How long does it take to be in ketosis?

This is a popular question among those who are just starting the ketogenic diet. It actually varies from two weeks or more. People with more insulin resistance usually take a longer time before they get to ketosis. Lean and young people usually get to ketosis faster.

Conclusion

This brings us to the end of our book. I know you have in one way or the other derived and gotten the perfect tools to help you go through your ketogenic diet challenge.

It is not that easy. It is like driving a car: at first, it is very hard to comprehend and the fear of crashing comes to mind. Then when you start driving, the road seems confusing. This book will serve as a tool you will use to perfectly know how to drive through the odds and get to the finish line.

When you start learning how to drive, you won't immediately know how to overtake, change lanes, and the uses of the devices in the car, how to reverse, and even to hit the horn. Everything is one after the other. Like I said earlier, *"the journey of a thousand miles begins with a step."* It is one step after the other and this book will help and guide you through this journey.

It has been a great pleasure for us to impart and flash the torch which points out the way to you. We are delighted that this book of ours has been a tool in modifying your life and taking you across the finish line of that journey of a thousand miles.

The ketogenic diet, if not the best, is one of the best ways in reducing body weight and excess fat. It was designed for the treatment of seizures, but unknown to mankind; it is like an onion of blessings. Within it, there are a lot of benefits and layers of treatment. It has been tested and trusted by many scientists all over the world.

Make sure you visit your doctor for you to be fit for this amazing treasure because an expert's point of view is also needed.

Thank you for reading our book today and make sure you also share this great treasure to everyone around because with this the world can be a better place. Let the ketogenic diet be a part of you because the ketogenic diet is not a diet, it is a lifestyle!

Show the world the lifestyle!

The Vegan-Keto Diet Meal Plan

Discover the Secrets to Amazing and Unexpected Uses for the Ketogenic Diet Plus Vegan Recipes and Essential Techniques to Get You Started

By: Amy Moore

Introduction:

Combining the Ketogenic Diet with Veganism

Welcome to the book that will change your life! If you're planning to follow the keto-vegan diet, then this book will help you understand both diets separately and how combining them is an excellent step towards a healthier lifestyle. Nowadays, it's important to make a conscious choice to start eating healthy. This will not only improve your overall health, but it will also enrich your life in ways you never thought possible.

These days, we hear about sicknesses, diseases, and illnesses caused by unhealthy eating habits and lifestyles. Our health has become a major problem—which is why people like you are taking steps to learn about healthy diets. The good news is, this book you've chosen is the best possible resource for you and here's why...

The keto-vegan diet is relatively new compared to all the other diet trends out there. But this book explains both diets in a simple, easy to comprehend way. This is very important, especially if this is your first time learning about the ketogenic diet, the vegan diet, and the keto-vegan diet—which is a winning combination. In this book, we first discuss the ketogenic diet and the vegan diet separately. We have presented the information this way to help you better understand why these diets are the trendiest ones in this modern day and age.

The first chapter is all about the ketogenic diet—what it is, how it works, the different types of keto diets, and what benefits you can gain from it. The second chapter focuses on veganism—what it is, what it means to go vegan, what the benefits are of going vegan, and how you can overcome the most common challenges of going vegan.

Now, you may be thinking to yourself, "Why is there a need to discuss these diets separately?"

The very important reason why it's important to learn about the ketogenic diet and the vegan diet separately is that this makes it easier for you to transition into the keto-vegan diet. As you will learn in this book, both diets are fairly restrictive. So if you start following the keto-vegan diet right away, this might cause quite a shock to your body. This is especially true if you're a big fan of carbs, meat, and dairy.

The good news is that you can start off by going vegan or going keto first. Then, when your body has gotten used to either diet, you can gradually incorporate the other one. This makes it easier for you to start with—and stick to—the keto-vegan diet. And since you will have already learned the fundamentals of the keto diet and the vegan diet in this book, you'll be all set to start your journey towards a healthy lifestyle! It's a simple, easy strategy that will help ensure your success.

Even if you're already following keto or you're already a vegan, this book will serve as a "refresher" course for you. It will also enable you to learn about the other half of the keto-vegan diet. And the best part is, there's more to learn!

Chapter three is where you will learn all about the keto-vegan diet. Here, you will find out why combining these two trendy—and highly effective—diets is a recipe for success. This chapter also talks about the benefits of this winning combination as well as some practical tips to help start you off. If you're planning to become a keto-vegan, this chapter will surely be of great help to you.

Speaking of great help, chapter four contains a wealth of information as well. Here, you will learn all about keto-vegan recipes. Before going into the recipes, you will first learn about the different types of foods you can eat—and those you should avoid—on the keto-vegan diet. Then it continues with ten different recipes which are simple, easy to make, healthy, and oh-so-tasty. Any of these mouthwatering recipes will help you stick with your diet while awakening your desire to make this diet part of your lifestyle.

As you will discover by reading the chapters in this book, the ketogenic diet and the vegan lifestyle are the most effective diets out there. Why do you think this diet combo is so popular right now? From celebrities to athletes and more, the keto-vegan diet is gaining momentum as the best—and it's only getting started. By reading this book, you have already taken that all-important first step. While a lot of people believe that the first step is to start following the diet, this isn't true. The first step is to make a conscious choice to learn all that you can about the diet/lifestyle you want to follow. After all, you won't be able to start following the keto-vegan diet properly—or any other type of diet, for that matter—unless you've learned all that you can about it.

This is especially true for the keto-vegan diet because it's a unique diet that involves a specific set of rules, particularly in terms of what you can and cannot eat. The more you learn about this diet, the easier it will be for you to start following it. And the more familiar you are with this diet—the more you understand it—the easier it will be for you to stick with the diet long-term. This is why making the choice to educate yourself is the "real" first step to take for any diet. While there are many resources online, it's difficult to sort through all the information and determine which ones are useful and which ones aren't accurate. The key is to find reliable, true information to guide you on your journey.

Fortunately for you, as far as books about the keto-vegan diet go, you've chosen a great one! And after learning all the basics about the keto-vegan diet and then some, you will be able to start your journey right away. This is a comprehensive book filled with practical information that you can easily apply to your life. It's time to say goodbye to your old, unhealthy eating habits. And it's time to start investing in your health!

Chapter 1: What Is the Ketogenic Diet

The simplest definition of the ketogenic diet is that it is a low-carb, high-fat, and moderate-protein diet. Ideally, when you follow this diet, only 10% of your total calories come from carbs, 20-30% of your total calories come from protein, and a whopping 60-70% of your total calories come from fats. The diet takes its name from its main goal—to reach a state of ketosis. After some time of following the keto diet, your body will start burning fats instead of glucose. This is why one of the main benefits of this diet—that also makes it extremely popular—is weight loss.

The macronutrient distribution of this diet requires you to eliminate foods that are high in carbs and sugar. One of the more controversial aspects of this diet is that it requires you to eliminate foods which were once thought to be healthy. This includes legumes, some types of fruits and vegetables, and even grains. However, you would be allowed to eat high-fat food items such as bacon, cheese, dairy, and more. When this diet first came onto the radar of health and fitness enthusiasts, it raised a lot of eyebrows. But as people saw proof of how effective the keto diet is—and as researchers studied it more—the world came to realize that it was more than just a trendy diet.

The only reason you would eliminate certain types of foods and food groups on the keto diet is that they are high in carbs. However, you would be replacing these foods with other types that will nourish you—and that fit into the keto diet. For instance, instead of eating a lot of starchy veggies, you would increase your intake of low-starch veggies such as leafy greens. You may also continue consuming veggies that contain moderate starch content such as carrots, red peppers, and more.

If you're a lover of veggies, there are things you can do to make them more keto-friendly. For one, you can cook your veggies in coconut oil, ghee, butter, and other healthy oils. This makes them taste better while helping you reach your daily fat recommendation on the keto diet. The keto diet also allows you to consume fish and meat without restriction—but for fish, it's recommended to go for the ones that contain healthy fats such as salmon, mackerel, anchovies, and herring. These are great options because they will not only help you consume enough fats, but they also contain other nutrients to keep you healthy. For meat, you may choose lean cuts once in a while, but the fatty cuts are better.

When it comes to following the keto diet—only the keto diet—the ratio between vegetables and meat that you consume depends on you. Generally, though, this diet requires more protein than high-carb diets. The key is to choose the types of foods you eat and try to avoid food items which are high in carbs and sugar.

On its own, the keto diet is pretty simple. It's fairly restrictive, especially in terms of carbs and sugar. This diet may also feel quite intimidating, especially at the beginning. In order to follow it correctly, you must learn how to count your macros. This enables you to ensure that you are getting the right amounts of fats, protein, and carbs to force your body into ketosis. Following the keto diet correctly is important. The good news is, there are different types of keto diets you can try depending on the macronutrient ratios you think you can handle.

How Does the Ketogenic Diet Work?

To help you understand how the ketogenic diet works, let us first review how the human body works—specifically how it produces energy. Most diets make our body run mainly on blood sugar or glucose which we get from carbs like potatoes, fruits, pasta, sweets, and bread. Most diets are also high in carbs—and people who don't follow specific diets tend to eat a lot of carbs. However, if our blood glucose levels drop, we feel our energy levels drop as well. The bad news is, our body isn't designed to store a lot of glucose. But the good news is that even if you don't consume a lot of carbs, your body can still function if it starts running on fats—and this happens when you reach ketosis.

While in a state of ketosis, your liver starts breaking down fats—the fats you consume and the fats stored in your body—into ketones or ketone bodies which are a usable source of energy. When this happens, your organs can start using these ketones to continue with their functions. Simply put, your body will become a fat-burning machine using fats instead of glucose as its main energy source. This process is considered adaptive as it occurs when you "starve" yourself of glucose by eliminating carbs and sugar from your diet.

As soon as your ketone levels increase, your body goes into ketosis. It starts burning fats—which is why the keto diet a very effective way to lose weight. There are a couple of ways you can achieve ketosis. One way is by fasting. This involves a cessation of eating for a long time period. There are some diets that involve fasting, the most popular of which is Intermittent Fasting or IF. Fasting forces your body into a state of ketosis as it starts burning fats for fuel in an attempt to decrease the amount of glucose it uses. This happens because you're "starving" your body of food.

Another effective way to reach ketosis is by following the keto diet. On this diet, you consume a lot of butter, eggs, cheese, meat, fish, oils, nuts, and veggies while avoiding bread, grains, legumes, beans, and a number of starchy fruits and vegetables. The nature of this diet is what forces your body into ketosis. You would be drastically limiting your carb intake—only eating enough to survive—while consuming high amounts of fats and moderate amounts of protein. To maintain ketosis, you need to consume a lot of fat since this is what your body will be using for fuel. It's also important to moderate your protein intake since protein can also be broken down by the body and converted into glucose. Therefore, if you consume more protein than what's recommended, you might not be able to reach and maintain ketosis.

Types of Ketogenic Diets

If you're planning to start the ketogenic diet (or the keto-vegan diet), one important thing to know about it is that there are different types of ketogenic diets you can choose from. This is great news because you have the option to choose the type of diet that fits your own lifestyle and health goals. The most common types of keto diets include:

- The Standard Ketogenic Diet (SKD)

The SKD is the most common type of keto diet—and it also happens to be the simplest one. The rule for this type of keto diet is very simple—all you have to do is consume a minimal amount of carbs all the time. For this diet, you would only be able to consume a maximum of 50 grams of carbs each day. The exact amount you consume depends on your own needs. This type of keto diet is suitable for most people.

- The Targeted Ketogenic Diet (TKD)

This type of diet allows you to eat more carbs compared to the other types. However, you should only consume these additional amounts of carbs right before working out. It's the preferred type of diet for athletes and for people who lead active lifestyles. Also, when choosing the additional carbs you plan to consume, it's best to opt for easily-digestible varieties so you don't end up with an upset stomach.

Although you would consume more carbs on this type of keto diet, you won't have to worry about not being able to achieve ketosis because you would effectively burn all those carbs during your workout. Although your state of ketosis would be disrupted, this won't happen for too long. Usually, you may consume up to 25 grams of additional carbs before your exercise routine. After working out, it's best to consume meals that are low in fat and high in protein. While the keto diet encourages you to eat a lot of fat, it's not recommended to consume fat after exercising. The reason for this is that it might weaken your muscle recovery and delay your body's absorption of nutrients.

It's important to note that this variation isn't suitable for everyone. If you live an active lifestyle or you have a daily workout routine, then this type of keto diet would be the best option for you. However, you must plan your meals well to ensure that you are not going beyond the recommended amounts of carbs and protein. Also, make sure that you're getting enough fats to maintain your state of ketosis.

- The Cyclic Ketogenic Diet (CKD)

This type of ketogenic diet is quite popular, especially with beginners. For this diet, you won't have to go completely go keto right away. The CKD involves cycling between "keto days" and "off days" each week. You would have alternate days of following the keto diet and days of consuming high amounts of carbs—this is called "carb-loading."

For this diet, you would have to consume a maximum of 50 grams of carbs each day on your keto days. Then on your off days, you may consume up to 600 grams of carbs while you're carb-loading. This type of keto diet is suitable for bodybuilders and other types of athletes who perform a lot of intense activities. It helps maximize fat loss while helping build lean mass. Like the TKD, this type of keto diet isn't recommended for most people.

- The Restricted Ketogenic Diet

This type of diet is recommended for therapeutic purposes—specifically for the management of certain types of cancer. Restricting your carb intake causes the body to start producing ketones. When this happens, the healthy cells of the body can start using ketones—but there are some types of cancer cells that can't run on this alternative energy source. Most types of cancer cells thrive on glucose. Therefore, starving yourself of glucose means that you're starving those cancer cells as well.

This variation of the keto diet is considered restricted because it's combined with caloric restriction thus making your body an inhospitable environment for cancer cells. For this diet, you would start by only consuming water for 3 to 5 days then continuing with the keto diet. For this diet, you would only consume a maximum of 20 grams of carbs. This type of diet is also recommended for those suffering from conditions like PCOS, chronic fatigue syndrome, various neurological diseases, and others. Also, you should only follow this diet under medical supervision to ensure your health and safety.

Now that you know more about the different types of keto diets, you can better determine which one suits you best. Knowing the type of keto diet to follow helps ensure your success—whether you plan to follow this diet on its own or incorporate another diet (like the vegan diet) into it. After choosing the type of diet to follow, you have the option to do more research about it. This will help you follow it correctly and get the most out of the ketogenic diet you have chosen.

The Benefits of the Keto Diet

The ketogenic diet isn't simply a low-carb diet. It also involves consuming high amounts of fat and moderate amounts of protein. Following the keto diet correctly allows you to reach a state of ketosis. Reaching this state is what provides all the excellent health benefits of the keto diet. If you plan to follow the keto diet or you have already been following it for some time now, here are some benefits to look forward to:

- It helps in the treatment of epilepsy

This is the main benefit of the ketogenic diet because it was actually developed for this purpose. Back in the 1900s, the ketogenic diet was created as part of the treatment for epilepsy. Until now, it's still being used for this purpose although even healthy individuals have started following it too for weight loss and for the other benefits the diet provides.

- It helps reduce your appetite

One of the most difficult challenges dieters face is feeling hungry all the time. When reducing portions or restricting certain foods from your diet, you feel like you're always hungry and you miss your favorite foods. But with the keto diet, you don't have to worry about this issue. Following a low-carb diet results in appetite reduction. The more protein and fat you eat, the fuller you feel—which means that you won't feel hungry all the time.

- It promotes weight loss

Since your body will start using fats—even your stored fats—as its main source of energy, this leads to weight loss as well. While following this diet, your insulin levels drop—insulin is a type of hormone that stores fat. This is what transforms your body into an efficient fat-burning machine.

When it comes to body fat, it's important to know that not all fat is the same. Fat stores in the body determine your risk of disease and how those fat stores affect your body. The two primary types of fat are subcutaneous—which can be found underneath the skin—and visceral—which is found in the abdominal cavity and around the organs. Insulin resistance and inflammation occur when you have excess visceral fat. Ketosis burns both fats which, in turn, helps you lose weight while reducing your risk of developing various medical conditions.

- It helps control blood sugar levels

Another benefit of the keto diet is that it helps naturally control your blood sugar levels. This occurs because of the types of foods you would consume while on this diet. This particular benefit makes the keto diet beneficial for people who suffer from diabetes. Whether you already suffer from this condition or you're at risk for it, you may want to consider following this diet.

- It improves your mental focus

After following the ketogenic diet for a few weeks or months, you may notice an improvement in your mental focus. The main reason for this is that ketones are an excellent fuel source for the brain. Also, consuming fewer carbs helps prevent spikes in your blood sugar levels. These effects lead to an improvement in concentration and focus. Furthermore, an increase in the consumption of fatty acids can have a positive effect on the functions of the brain.

- It increases your energy levels

Ketones are a more reliable source of energy for the body. Unlike glucose which gets depleted easily, the energy provided by fats lasts for longer periods of time. Therefore, you may start noticing an increase in your energy levels as one of the benefits of this diet.

- It improves the levels of good cholesterol and triglycerides

Studies have shown that this diet can improve good cholesterol and triglyceride levels that are commonly associated with arterial accumulation. This diet increases HDL levels while decreasing LDL levels. It also improves blood pressure compared to other types of diets.

- It may help reduce acne

Switching to a keto diet can also help improve the health and condition of your skin. You may notice a reduction in your acne along with a reduction in skin inflammation. Some studies have suggested that consuming a lot of carbs may lead to an increase in acne, therefore, following the low-carb keto diet will improve this skin condition.

To improve this benefit further, you may want to follow a cleaning regimen strictly as well.

- It may be helpful against Metabolic Syndrome

Metabolic Syndrome or MS is a medical condition that's commonly associated with a risk of heart disease and diabetes. MS isn't a single condition—it's a collection of symptoms including high blood pressure, high triglycerides, low HDL levels, abdominal obesity, and elevated blood sugar levels. The good news is that the ketogenic diet improves all of these, thus, it may help improve MS.

Chapter 2: What is the Vegan Diet?

The vegan diet—or veganism—is a type of diet/lifestyle that involves the exclusion of animals (meat) and animal products such as dairy, eggs, and more from the diet. A lot of vegans also avoid foods that have been processed using animal products—like some types of wine and refined sugar.

If you have chosen to make veganism your lifestyle, you would be known as a vegan. A vegan is a person who follows the vegan diet, but the term can also be used as an adjective to describe a certain dish or food item. While some vegans only avoid consuming animals and animal products, there are others who go further by avoiding animal-based or animal-derived commercial products such as wool, fur, makeup, and others. There are different types of vegans who have varying levels of strictness in terms of how they follow this lifestyle. These types are:

- **Dietary vegans** are also known as "plant-based eaters." They avoid consuming animal products, but they continue using animal products like cosmetics and clothing.

- **Junk food vegans** aren't really concerned with their health as they rely mostly on heavily-processed vegan options. If you plan to go vegan, you may want to avoid being this type of vegan.

- **Raw food vegans** only consume plant-based food sources that are either raw or that have been cooked at temperatures lower than 118°F.

- **Raw food, low-fat vegans** are also called "fruitarians." They rely mainly on fruits and only consume foods which are high in fats such as avocados, coconuts, different types of nuts, and more. However, they do consume other types of plants in small amounts too, but only once in a while.

- **Whole-food vegans** avoid all animal and animal products as well, but they prefer consuming whole foods such as nuts, seeds, legumes, fruits, veggies, and whole grains.

If you're reading this book, it means that you're interested in becoming a keto-vegan. This is a fairly new type of vegan who combines the basic rules of the vegan diet with those of the ketogenic diet. In other words, you would be following a ketogenic plant-based diet. Later on, we will discuss this diet combination further.

These days, becoming a vegan isn't as challenging as it was in the past. Nowadays, veganism has become a trend. Because of this, more and more vegan options are being made available to people who would like to follow this healthy and beneficial diet. Even if you started out as a lover of meat, vegan-friendly substitutes these days taste just like the real thing. This would make it easier for you to transition into the vegan diet.

While some people can easily stop eating meat and other animal products, there are others who struggle with it—even with all of the vegan-friendly options available. After all, this diet differs significantly from other diets, especially if you follow a diet that includes a lot of meat. In fact, the keto diet allows you to eat meat and other animal products. So if you start by going vegan, you still have to make some significant changes to become a keto-vegan.

The good news is that transitioning from the vegan diet to the keto vegan diet—or from the keto diet to the keto-vegan diet—isn't just possible, it's quite easy to accomplish as long as you know how to do it. Of course, the more liberal you are as a vegan, the easier it will be for you to transition into the keto-vegan diet. But even if you're following a very strict vegan diet, making this shift is still possible. It's all about making a commitment to the diet/lifestyle you have chosen in order to reach your long-term goals.

What Does it Mean to Be a Vegan

Veganism is more of a lifestyle than a diet—especially according to those who have adopted veganism as part of their life. Going vegan can help you become healthier compared to those who consume a lot of animals and animal products. As a vegan, you wouldn't consume meat (both white and red), fish, seafood, dairy products, eggs, or other animal products such as honey. This also means that as a vegan, you wouldn't be consuming cholesterol, animal fats, and animal proteins—all of which may cause damage to your health. Instead, you would survive on healthy, whole foods that contain vitamins, minerals, fiber, protein, good fats, and complex carbohydrates. People choose to go vegan for different reasons including:

- Environment

Veganism can potentially help save the environment—that is if a majority of the people in the world choose to go vegan. Choosing the vegan diet (and other plant-based diets) can have a positive effect on the environment, especially in terms of animal agriculture. Consuming more plant-based foods can lower the need for resources that cause high amounts of greenhouse-gas emissions. Also, this diet isn't as water-intensive as diets that require animal agriculture. This means that people who would like to contribute to saving the environment may have this as their main reason for going vegan.

- Ethics

When people adopt veganism because of ethical reasons, they do so because they have a strong belief in the rights of all living things to freedom and to life. They make a conscious choice to eliminate animals and animal products from their diet as well as from their life. Also, ethical vegans don't agree with the physical and psychological trauma that the animals in different industries endure. Animals raised for meat or other purposes are forced to live their lives in deplorable and miserable conditions before they are cruelly slaughtered for the benefit of human beings. Aside from going vegan, they may also express their opposition by raising awareness, protesting, and trying to convince others to adopt the same lifestyle as them.

- Health

These days, health is a very common reason why people choose to go vegan. The vegan diet does offer a lot of significant health benefits, which we will be discussing in a bit. Apart from these health benefits, some people choose the vegan lifestyle because they want to avoid the adverse side effects linked to the hormones, antibiotics, and chemicals used in the animal food industry. But out of all the health reasons, the most common one that convinces people to go vegan is weight loss.

No matter what your reason is for going vegan, this choice will surely change your life. The vegan diet can help you become a healthier and more well-rounded person. This is what it means to be a vegan—and this is why more and more people have made the choice to become part of this growing trend.

The Benefits of Going Vegan

While you may hear a lot of vegans saying that they've chosen veganism to save animals and other living things, there are other benefits you may enjoy when you choose to go vegan. If you plan to follow the vegan diet or you have already been following it for some time now, here are some benefits to look forward to:

- It provides excellent nutritional value

Several studies and researchers have shown that when you follow the vegan diet correctly, you would be consuming a lot of vitamins, minerals, antioxidants, and nutrients. But while the vegan diet is chock-full of these healthy nutrients, it does lack meat—a very important source of protein. Therefore, if you plan to follow the vegan diet, you must make sure that you consume a lot of plant-based protein sources so that you don't end up becoming protein deficient. Another nutrient you might end up being deficient in is iron. Therefore, you must consume a lot of iron-rich plant-based sources as well. Other than these nutrients, veganism can be extremely beneficial to your overall health.

- It may help improve your mood

Research suggests that vegans may be significantly happier than those who consume animals and animal products. This may be due to the fact that plant-based foods are fresher and healthier than animal-based ones. So when you mainly consume such foods, it helps purify your mind to maintain positivity.

- It may help in the prevention of various diseases

Since plant-based food sources don't contain a lot of saturated fats, veganism may help reduce the risk of developing heart disease. This diet also plays an important role in the prevention of various diseases such as diabetes, hypertension, some forms of cancer, gallstones, and more.

- It may improve kidney function while lowering blood sugar levels

Veganism may help lower your blood sugar levels. This is a good thing whether you're healthy or you suffer from some kind of medical condition. This benefit may also lower your risk of developing diabetes. Following this diet may improve your kidney function which, in turn, helps improve your overall health.

- It may reduce the frequency of migraines you experience

Migraines can be very difficult to deal with, especially if they happen frequently. Fortunately, this is one benefit offered by veganism. Following this diet may help reduce the onset of migraines. Often, food is a trigger for migraines, therefore, if you change your diet to a healthier one, you might notice that you don't experience migraines as much.

- It may protect you against some forms of cancer

One significant factor that may help reduce the risk of developing cancer is your diet. As with the keto diet, following the vegan diet means eliminating foods that commonly serve as food for cancer cells. This is especially true if you opt for fresh, whole foods rather than processed or packaged foods which are commonly found in diets that include meat and other animal products.

- It promotes weight loss

This is one of the most popular reasons why people choose the vegan lifestyle—to lose weight. These days, people all over the world are focused on losing weight either for health reasons or to improve their self-confidence. But for this benefit, you have to follow the vegan diet properly. Just because you eat plant-based food sources, this doesn't guarantee that you will lose weight. For instance, if all you consume are vegan fast foods and vegan junk foods, you shouldn't expect to shed those unwanted pounds anytime soon. Therefore, if you want to enjoy this benefit, make smart choices when it comes to choosing your plant-based food sources.

- It helps improve athletic performance

While athletic performance requires an adequate protein intake, the vegan diet may help improve your athletic performance as well. Following a nutrient-rich vegan diet allows you to become stronger and healthier to allow for optimum performance at sports. This is why more and more athletes are making the choice to go vegan—it makes them feel better and it makes them perform better too.

- It may help reduce arthritic pain

Some studies have shown that this diet also has a positive impact on people who suffer from different kinds of arthritis. Following this diet may reduce the pain and swelling caused by the condition which, in turn, allows for better mobility and general functioning of the affected areas.

- It helps balance hormones

There are certain hormones in the body that can cause adverse effects when their levels become too high. One example of such a hormone is estrogen which can contribute to the development of breast cancer—and the production of this hormone may increase due to the consumption of animal fats. Because the vegan diet promotes the consumption of nutrient-dense, whole foods, this can help balance the body's hormones to ensure optimum function at all times.

- It will make you live longer

Finally, veganism may also allow you to enjoy a healthier and longer life compared to those who consume a lot of meat. As with all the other benefits, this one comes from the nature of the diet and the kinds of food you would consume while following it.

How to Overcome Challenges as a Vegan

Nowadays, there is a growing trend for plant-based diets such as the vegan diet. Although it's easier to become a vegan now compared to the past, this doesn't mean that going vegan doesn't come with its own challenges. Apart from this diet being significantly different from the traditional diet that includes a lot of meat, dairy, eggs, and more, there are some other issues you might encounter on your journey towards becoming a vegan. Let's go through the most common of these issues—and how to help you overcome them:

1. Dining out

Although this might not seem like such a big deal at first, you will come to discover that being a vegan who dines out frequently can be quite challenging. For one, not all restaurants are vegan-friendly. If the people you dine out with don't know that you're vegan, they'll just choose any restaurant they want to dine at—and you will be left with a conundrum. Do you break your diet "just this once" or do you simply order a side salad to stick with your new diet?

For the first option, giving in "just this once" can easily become a habit. Soon, you'll realize that you've been breaking your diet frequently without even noticing it. For the second option, ordering something that doesn't make you feel full or satisfied probably won't make you feel happy about yourself. Also, not telling the people you dine with that you're vegan would lead to this kind of situation happening often.

On the other hand, if you do tell your friends about your new diet, they might react in different ways. If you have friends who are open-minded, they will accept your lifestyle choice and do their best to accommodate you. This is great news for you because you will be able to dine at restaurants that offer vegan-friendly options. But what if your friends aren't too happy about the fact that you've gone vegan? In such a case, you might notice that dinner invitations are becoming less frequent. This is a sad reality that some vegans have to face.

If you don't want such a situation to happen to you, the best thing you can do is to assure your friends that you will neither talk about veganism all night nor force them to go vegan just like you. Also, you can be more proactive in terms of deciding which restaurant to go to. Do your research and find out which establishments in your area offer vegan dishes. Then you can make suggestions to dine at these establishments once in a while. Or if your friends want to dine somewhere that isn't completely vegan-friendly, you can check their menu beforehand to see what options you have. Chances are, there will be some dishes that will fit into your diet. Checking the menu makes it easier to decide if you can join your friends or if it would be better to take a rain check so you don't have to deal with an awkward situation.

2. Attending parties and other social events

Another challenging—and common—situation is to attend non-vegan parties as a vegan. Once news gets around that you're a vegan, some people might feel worried about inviting you. The good news is that this issue is quite easy to overcome. First, assure your family, friends, and acquaintances that they don't have to make changes to their plans just to accommodate your new diet. Tell them that you're totally okay with attending parties with non-vegans.

You can even offer to bring a vegan dish to share with everyone. The key here is to approach the situation as open-mindedly and as positively as possible. That way, the people around you don't feel intimidated by your lifestyle choice and they won't hesitate to send you an invitation when they're planning parties.

3. Traveling

Traveling is another challenging situation, especially in the beginning. The more you travel and the longer you stick with veganism, the more you will get the hang of traveling as a vegan. But for the first few times you travel, you may feel a lot of temptation to break your diet—at least for the duration of the trip.

This temptation won't just come from the fact that new places offer new and exciting dishes that you would like to try. It would also come from the fact that you're going to a new place you know nothing about. So how do you overcome this issue?

Through research. Before traveling, do research about the place you are traveling to. Go online and search for vegan restaurants, shops, and establishments in the area. Chances are, you will be able to find a good number of places that offer vegan fare. Also, you may want to consider packing vegan foods—especially snacks—for your trip. That way, even if you end up in a place that doesn't have a lot of vegan-friendly food options, you won't end up going hungry.

4. Non-acceptance from family and friends

This is one issue that can be very challenging to deal with. Challenging—but not impossible. If you come from a long line of meat eaters and you suddenly decide to go vegan, the people around you won't understand why you would ever make this choice. They might ask you a lot of questions, ridicule you, and generally, make you feel bad about your decision.

Don't give up and don't start a fight with them either. Going vegan isn't something you should destroy your relationships over. Instead, give them some time to process what you've said. After some time, you can open up the topic with them again. Explain your reason for becoming a vegan in a positive way. Also, assure them that you don't expect them to go vegan, neither do you expect them to make changes in their lives just to accommodate you. Tell them that this is your choice and your change—this means that they don't have to make any changes in their life just to accommodate you.

To avoid conflict, try to be as positive and accepting as you can be. Expect them to react negatively and prepare for it. Show them that you understand where they are coming from, you accept their opinions, and you respect them for who they are. Hopefully, this will change their attitude towards you—and towards veganism too, especially when they see how your new lifestyle is benefitting you in so many ways.

5. Explaining your lifestyle choice without offending others

For non-vegans, there's nothing worse than hearing vegans talk about how the vegan lifestyle is healthier and much more ethical than theirs. Hearing vegans go on and on about how veganism is the best diet out there can be quite offensive—especially if they already have a negative perception about veganism and vegans.

Have you ever heard the expression, "less words, less mistakes" before? This expression applies perfectly to this situation. There's no need to preach about veganism unless someone asks you about it. If one of your friends and family members asks you about your vegan journey, then you can share your story in a simple and positive way. If they ask more questions or they seem genuinely interested in veganism, then you may continue sharing information. But it's not really a good idea to open up the topic, especially at gatherings and other social events where the majority of guests are non-vegans.

When explaining veganism to others, try not to make them feel guilty about their own diets or lifestyles. Doing this causes others to adopt a defensive attitude which might cause them to feel even more negatively towards veganism. Instead, talk about your own personal journey and how veganism makes you feel good about yourself. You can even share some of the challenges you have faced and how to overcome them. This makes your journey more realistic and relatable compared to when you just gush about veganism to people who don't have the same views and opinions as yourself.

Chapter 3: Can Vegans Follow the Keto Diet Too?

These days, more and more people are going vegan to lose weight. Of course, there are also a good number of vegans out there who have chosen this lifestyle because of their ethics and beliefs. However, this isn't the only trendy diet these days—there are many more. Because of this, vegans who have chosen the lifestyle for its health benefits are starting to look for ways to improve their diets further. This is how the keto-vegan diet began. It's a variation of the ketogenic diet which is starting to draw a lot of attention from health enthusiasts all over the world.

As previously mentioned, the main goal of the ketogenic diet is to force the body to shift its primary fuel source. Following the ketogenic diet causes the body to start burning fat instead of glucose. Since the keto diet became popular, more and more people—specifically vegans—are wondering if it's okay for them to follow the keto diet too.

The simple answer to this is—yes, vegans can follow the ketogenic diet too. In fact, combining their current vegan lifestyle with the keto diet can actually enhance the health benefits they are already experiencing, especially in terms of weight loss.

For some vegans, they wonder why they aren't losing weight even though they had been following veganism for a significant amount of time. The main reason for this is that, although this diet focuses on eating mainly veggies and fruits, it tends to be more fat-deficient and carb-heavy compared to other diets. Unfortunately, consuming a lot of carbs can lead to weight gain or it might not help you lose weight as quickly as you had hoped. Therefore, if you really want to lose weight on the vegan diet, you should be smart in terms of choosing the right types of fruits and vegetables to eat.

Or you can also combine veganism with the keto diet to help you reach your weight-loss goals a lot faster.

While it's okay for vegans to follow the ketogenic diet too, it's best to learn everything that you can before starting this beneficial combination. Think about it—did you simply make a choice to become a vegan then start following the diet the very next day?

Probably not.

You would have first learned more about the vegan diet, how it works, what it entails, and how to follow it correctly. After learning all this, that's the time when you would have started the diet. The same thing applies to the keto-vegan diet. Learn all you can about it first, make a plan, and start following it. Fortunately, you have this book to guide you. Now that you have learned more about the ketogenic diet and the vegan diet, it's time to learn more about how these diets work in tandem with one another.

When you first try to think of both diets, you might not see how they would work together. After all, the keto diet focuses more on high-fat food items like bacon, eggs, cheese, and the like. But on the vegan diet, you focus on plant-based foods. So, how does the combination work? Let's find out...

Keto-Vegan - A Winning Combination

The keto-vegan diet isn't just possible—it already exists and it's being followed by more and more people all over the world. This means that as a vegan, you can start following the keto diet. Or as a follower of the ketogenic diet, you can combine this with the vegan diet as well.

Even if you follow neither of these diets, you also have the option to start following both diets simultaneously.

But while this is possible, the keto-vegan diet does come with some very unique challenges. One of the main challenges people face when it comes to this diet is how restrictive it can be. The keto diet restricts sugar in all forms along with foods that contain high amounts of carbs while the vegan diet restricts all meat and animal products. This means that you would have to survive on a very specific list of food items that would suit both diets. While this might seem like an issue to a lot of people, it doesn't have to be.

Why?

Because despite all of the types of food you must eliminate from your diet, there is still a wide range of food items you can choose from. Instead of thinking of the keto-vegan diet as a restrictive diet, you can think of it as a low-carb, plant-based diet that will help you achieve your health and weight-loss goals.

Whether you have chosen to go vegan because of ethical or health reasons, when you consider the way animals are raised in the food industry these days, you would realize that there are very good reasons to start shifting your focus to plant-based fats. Following a plant-based diet allows you to consume more antioxidants, vitamins, and minerals each day which, in turn, provides anti-inflammatory effects for your body. Also, eating less animal-based protein can help slow cancer growth.

We have already gone through the different benefits of the ketogenic diet and the vegan diet separately. But you may have noticed that both diets share similar benefits. Therefore, it only makes sense that when you combine these diets, you enhance the benefits they provide.

The most important goal of veganism is to eliminate animals and animal byproducts from your diet—then replace these with plant-based sources. But in order to lose weight and enjoy all the other benefits of this diet, you should be able to choose the proper types of food to eat. Consider this—if you go vegan but all you eat are processed vegan foods, vegan fast food, vegan desserts, and vegan junk food, it's highly unlikely that you will experience all the benefits of this diet.

This is where keto comes in. Incorporating the ketogenic diet into your existing vegan diet means that you would eliminate the unhealthy foods from your diet—specifically sugars and simple carbs. Doing this will have a huge effect on your health and your waistline. Eliminating these food items will force your body to enter ketosis thus becoming an efficient fat-burning machine.

The keto-vegan diet is considered a winning combination because it goes either way. If you start with keto, you might be in danger of eating excessive amounts of fats—bad fats—if you focus on processed meats, trans fats, and other unhealthy options. But combine this with the vegan diet and you will be able to enjoy the benefits of both diets together.

The Benefits of Becoming a Keto-Vegan

Anyone who follows the keto-vegan diet has their own health goals in mind. You may have your reasons for choosing to follow this diet combination and now that you know more about it, you may feel more determined to start. To encourage you even more, here are the health benefits of the keto-vegan diet that you can look forward to:

- To maintain a healthy weight

Most people who have started on the keto diet have done so in order to lose weight. One of the biggest struggles dieters face is to reach their target goals and maintain a healthy weight. By combining the keto diet with veganism, you will focus on eating high amounts of plant-based fats, moderate amounts of plant-based protein, and minimal amounts of plant-based carbs.

Since everything you eat will be plant-based, you will be able to lose weight a lot faster. This is especially beneficial if you are overweight or obese. As your body enters ketosis, it will start burning your fat stores thus helping you reach your target weight faster. And the best part is, you will be able to maintain a healthy weight as long as you continue with this diet combination.

- To combat or prevent diabetes

The keto-vegan diet minimizes your carb intake while eliminating sugar—the two types of food that cause diabetes. Therefore, this diet can help you combat or even prevent the development of diabetes. If you already suffer from diabetes, the diet helps lower your blood sugar levels allowing you to manage your condition more effectively.

Over time, you may be able to lower your insulin doses or even completely eliminate your medications depending on how severe your condition is. One thing to keep in mind if you suffer from this condition is to consult with your doctor regularly. This allows your doctor to monitor your condition and determine how the diet is affecting you. Also, your doctor is the best person to recommend the lowering of your medication doses or the elimination of your medications completely.

- To give you more energy

When your body burns carbs for energy, it gives you energy for a while but it eventually gets depleted. On the other hand, if your body burns fats for energy—which is what will happen on the keto-vegan diet—the energy you get will last for longer periods of time. This means that it will give you more energy and a consistent supply of energy rather than spikes of energy that don't last long.

- To lower the risk of heart disease

One of the main causes of death all over the world is heart disease which can be caused by different factors. On a keto-vegan diet, you will be consuming a lot of healthy fats which are good for your heart. This diet reduces the fat molecules that circulate in your bloodstream which may cause heart disease. Also, consuming too many carbs causes an increase in triglycerides which, eventually, may lead to heart disease. Since keto-vegan is a low-carb diet, you don't have to worry about this issue.

- To improve the overall health of your brain

The keto-vegan diet also helps enhance mental cognition. This helps improve your focus as well as your critical thinking skills. Following this diet combination maintains the health and sharpness of your brain. The keto-vegan diet is a balanced diet that's low in carbs, high in good fats, and moderate in plant-based proteins. The nature of this diet helps prevent the accumulation of beta-amyloid protein—a type of protein that hinders the flow of brain signals. This benefit helps reduce the risk of developing Alzheimer's Disease, Parkinson's Disease, and other neurodegenerative conditions.

- To combat some types of cancer

Unfortunately, there is no cure for cancer. The best thing you can do is try to prevent it from developing. Fortunately, the keto-vegan diet does just that—it can help maintain optimal metabolic functions in the body to combat some types of cancer. Studies have shown that cancer cells love meat and sugar. Since you will eliminate these food items from your diet, you will also be reducing your risk of developing this deadly condition. This diet also protects your body by minimizing your carb intake and replacing this with healthy fats. Doing this starves the cancer cells so they can't thrive, grow, or reproduce.

- To help improve the health of the eyes

There are several eye-related progressive diseases that can cause poor vision or blindness. But through the keto-vegan diet, you can improve the health of your eyes in order to prevent such diseases. This diet improves the health of retinal cells and it also prevents the degeneration of cells. Even if you already suffer from conditions like glaucoma or cataracts, this diet may slow down or stop your condition from getting worse.

- To improve gut health

This diet promotes a healthy and diverse gut microbiome. This is essential because when you have a lot of good, healthy bacteria, your body is able to absorb nutrients and fats more effectively and at a faster rate. Good bacteria help maintain the health of the intestinal lining which, in turn, helps break down foods while stimulating the absorption of nutrients. There are also specific types of gut bacteria that help provide vitamin K and vitamin B12 which help regulate the minerals in the body. The keto-vegan diet also promotes a healthy metabolism—and this leads to disease and weight gain prevention.

- To stabilize your hormone levels

Your hormones are your body's chemical messengers. Therefore, if any hormone imbalances occur inside your body, this might lead to chaotic and harmful results. The good news is that ketosis has a positive effect on your hormone levels. When you reach a state of ketosis, this lowers your insulin levels. Leptin levels go down as well, and this causes a reduction in your appetite and cravings. For women, the keto-vegan diet improves the function of the pituitary gland. It also regulates the production of progesterone and the function of the thyroid gland.

- To make your skin healthier and clearer

This benefit comes from the reduction of carbs and dairy products in the body. These food items may cause inflammation which is one of the most common factors that cause acne. Consuming a lot of sugar can also cause breakouts and severe cases of acne. While carbs and sugar have adverse effects on the skin, good fats prevent inflammatory acne and have a soothing effect on dry skin. This is yet another benefit to look forward to once you start following the keto-vegan diet.

- To improve sleep

The keto-vegan diet also improves the quality of your sleep. This is very important since your body's recovery processes occur while you're sleeping. When you stick with this diet, it will provide the energy levels you need throughout the day and when night time comes, it helps you fall asleep—and stay asleep throughout the night. As you reduce the amount of carbs you consume while increasing the amount of healthy fats, this causes a change in your sleep patterns. According to researchers, the keto-vegan diet has a positive effect on the production of adenosine—a type of brain chemical that helps in sleep regulation.

Tips for Following the Keto-Vegan Diet Combination

For a lot of people, the keto-vegan diet may seem overwhelming. This is especially true for those who consume virtually anything placed in front of them. But for those who know better—like you and those who actually follow the diet—it's not that difficult to follow. The fact is, even though you would have to eliminate different kinds of food from your diet, this doesn't mean that you will have to eat unappealing, bland, or boring foods for the rest of your life.

It's all about knowing what kinds of food you can eat and realizing that these options are not only healthier, but they also provide you with a wide range of new and interesting flavors you're probably not used to having. As with any new diet or eating plan, the keto-vegan diet will take some getting used to. But as long as you learn the fundamentals of the diet and come up with a plan for how you will follow it, there's no reason why you won't be successful at adopting the keto-vegan lifestyle.

Although the keto-vegan diet may seem difficult, it doesn't have to be. The key is to know what foods to eliminate and what foods you should eat to replace them. This means that you have to start filling up on plant-based fats and proteins while trying to stay away from high-carb, plant-based sources. Here are some other tips and strategies to help you follow—and stick with—this diet:

1. Most of your carb intake will come from veggies—and this is a good thing

Simply going keto comes with a temptation to consume a lot of high-fat foods that aren't healthy such as junk food, processed food, fast food, and more. Although these types of food items may contribute to your daily fat intake, they aren't the right types of fats. But when you shift to plant-based food sources, you're sure to get the healthy fats that will provide you with all the benefits of this diet.

In the same way, you should also shift your carb intake from consuming unhealthy carbs to getting these carbs from vegetables. The great thing about getting most of your carbs from veggies is that these veggies also contain other essential nutrients. Although you will generally have to avoid starchy vegetables (and fruits), you can still indulge in these once in a while to help you reach your daily carb requirement. Just be smart when it comes to consuming veggies that contain a lot of carbs—make sure you know the carb content of these veggies so you can stick to the recommended amount each day.

2. Recognize the versatility of tofu

Tofu is considered a staple food on the keto-vegan diet. Eliminating meat, fish, and other high-protein sources might make you feel hungry. The good news is that you can use tofu to replace these foods. Tofu is an excellent substitute for meat. There are different types of tofu available and you can use them for different types of dishes. If you're not a fan of tofu, other great meat substitutes are tempeh and seitan.

3. You might not have a lot of variety... unless you

make an effort

The first time you think about the foods to eliminate on the keto-vegan diet, you might start feeling hopeless. Imagine—you would have to totally eliminate dairy, eggs, meat, grains, and even fruits and veggies that are high in carbs. After eliminating all of these, it may seem like there's not much left... right?

Wrong.

The key is to make an effort in terms of finding what types of food you can eat. Don't just focus on the foods to limit, avoid, or eliminate. Instead, focus on the foods that are recommended on the keto-vegan diet. In the next chapter, you will discover a comprehensive list of these foods. After reading the list, you will come to realize that there are a lot of options to choose from. With all these available options, all you have to do is mix things up, search for keto-vegan recipes, and start enjoying this new diet more.

4. Clean-up your pantry and stock up!

It's extremely difficult to start a new diet when your home is chock full of food items that you're not allowed to eat. After a few days, you might end up giving in to temptation and consuming those steaks in your refrigerator. If you want to succeed, you must prepare for it. Before you start your keto-vegan diet, you should first clean up your pantry, kitchen, and refrigerator. Get rid of all the food items that don't fit into your new diet. You don't have to throw these items away—you can either consume them (if you don't have a lot) or give them away to friends and family. If you choose the latter, make sure that the food items you give away haven't passed their expiration dates yet.

After cleaning up, you may want to visit your local grocery stores, farmers markets, and food shops. Check out available food items that you can eat while on the keto-vegan diet. While you're still learning, you can print out a list of all the foods you're allowed to eat. Then bring this list with you when shopping for food. Then take note of the shops that offer these food items so you know where to go when it's time to restock your pantry.

5. Give meal planning a try

One of the most common reasons why people fail when they start new diets is that they're too busy. Therefore, they end up going for the more convenient options—pre-packed, prepared, and processed foods. Unfortunately, since the keto-vegan diet is relatively new, there's a very small chance that you will find food options that are both healthy and suitable for this diet.

To overcome this issue, you may want to consider meal planning. This involves setting one to two days each week to plan, prepare, and cook your meals for the whole week. For instance, if you work from Monday to Friday, you can set your planning and shopping day on Saturday while you prepare and cook all your meals for the week on Sunday. Meal planning may take some getting used to—but once you get the hang of it, you'll discover that it saves you a lot of time, money, and it also helps you stick with your diet. When you have ready-made meals that you have made yourself, you won't have an excuse to go for those unhealthy yet highly convenient options that will cause you to deviate from your keto-vegan lifestyle.

6. When it comes to fatty oils—choose wisely

While half of the keto-vegan diet is all about consuming high amounts of fat, you must choose your fats and fat sources wisely too, especially in terms of fatty oils. Whether you use the oils for cooking or to add to your meals, the best types are MCT oil, coconut oil, and avocado oil. Among these oils, coconut oil is the most recommended because, according to new research, it may help you maintain ketosis for a longer time and it also targets belly fat in terms of fat-burning.

7. Don't do too many things too fast

If this is your first time starting a diet, you might want to ease into it gradually. Remember—the keto-vegan diet is fairly restrictive. If you immediately eliminate several food categories from your diet, you might end up struggling. This is especially true if these categories include your favorite foods. If you want to increase your chances of success, you should take things slowly. You may want to start with either diet first then gradually incorporate the other. If you want to start the keto-vegan diet right away, do so by eliminating the food categories one at a time. This way, you're already making an effort, but you're not causing too much stress on your body and mind.

8. Make sure you aren't developing nutrient deficiencies

One common issue dieters face is developing nutrient deficiencies. This is a common issue with diets that eliminate certain food groups. Speak to your doctor about this diet you're planning to start. Do this even if you're at the peak of health. Talk to your doctor about potentially developing nutrient deficiencies and ask if you need to take vitamin supplements to avoid this issue. But if you know how to balance your diet and choose the right foods, you may not have to worry about this issue. This is why it's important to learn about the diet—so you know exactly how to follow it without compromising your health.

9. Learn how to customize your keto-vegan diet

When it comes to the keto-vegan diet, remember that there is no "one-size-fits-all" plan to follow. Don't believe online sites and resources claiming that they have the "perfect plan" for you. If you really want to follow this diet, you must customize it according to your own needs and preferences. There's no point in following a diet plan when you don't like half of the suggested meals or recipes. You're the best person to create your own keto-vegan diet plan. In the beginning, you may have to experiment with different foods, dishes, and recipes. The longer you follow the diet, the more you will discover what you like and what you don't like. Don't be afraid of flexibility. Change things up once in a while. Customizing your own keto-diet plan enables you to control your own food choices. This helps you feel more motivated to keep with the diet long-term.

10. After some time, consider trying the raw keto-vegan diet

After following the keto-vegan diet successfully for some time, you may be interested in improving its health benefits. To do this, you may want to consider the raw version of the keto-vegan diet. Shifting to this version isn't difficult—all you have to do is consume seeds, nuts, and veggies raw instead of cooking them. You don't have to do this—it's just a suggestion for those who want to make things easier and healthier. But if you're happy with how the "normal" keto-vegan diet is working for you, then you can continue following it.

Chapter 4: Keto-Vegan Recipes

Once you've started your keto-vegan journey, you might start feeling that everything is off-limits. This is especially true if you shifted from being a non-vegan who loves carbs. While the keto-vegan diet is fairly restrictive, this doesn't mean that you can't enjoy good food while following it. As long as you know what to eat and where to find these food items, you don't have to feel sorry for yourself all the time. In fact, there are so many food items to choose from and a variety of dishes you can whip up that are healthy and will tickle your taste buds in surprising new ways.

What Types of Keto Foods Can Vegans Eat?

There are certain types of food you should eat while following the keto diet. In the same way, there are certain types of food you should eat while following the vegan diet. When you put these two diets together, there are certain things you should be eating while following the keto-vegan diet. Since you will be combining two diets which have a degree of restrictiveness, you may have to do some planning in order to successfully follow this diet combination. To remind you, here are some basic rules:

- You shouldn't consume any animal products.
- Increase your intake of high-fat food items, low-carb veggies, and leafy greens.
- Limit your carb and sugar intake.
- Obtain your protein from plant-based sources.
- Avoid processed food items.

There are different ways to start following the keto-vegan diet. The easier ways are to start by going either vegan or keto then gradually incorporate the other diet. But you also have the choice to immediately step into a keto-vegan diet journey though this will be a lot more challenging. One of the main concerns while following this diet is where to get your protein. While keto is a high-fat, low-carb diet, you must also consume moderate amounts of protein to remain healthy and strong. To help you out, here are some of the best plant-based protein sources to add to your diet:

- Macadamia Nuts and Almonds

Although nuts are healthy, not all types of nuts are suitable for your keto-vegan diet. This is mainly because there are several types that are high in carbs and it's very easy to go overboard when snacking on them or adding nuts to dishes. If you really want to keep on eating nuts, it's best to go for macadamia nuts and almonds.

- Meat Substitutes

There are a few options for low-carb meat substitutes that you can consume as part of your keto-vegan diet. These options are tasty, versatile, and practical too. Some good examples are tofu, tempeh, and seitan.

- Nutritional Yeast

This is a type of seasoning that is mainly used as an alternative in dishes—it's most commonly used to replace parmesan cheese. Nutritional yeast has a cheesy, nutty flavor, making it an excellent addition to savory dishes.

It's low-carb, high in protein, and its versatility makes it quite popular.

- Protein Powders

Adding protein powders to your diet is a great way to ensure that you're consuming enough protein each day. Just make sure that the protein powders you choose are keto-friendly too. Check the label (or product specifications if you're ordering online) to make sure that it fits into your new diet.

- Spinach

Surprising as this may seem, this leafy green contains good amounts of protein, especially when compared to other leafy greens. You can add spinach to your dishes and make raw spinach the main component when eating salads. Apart from protein, spinach also contains other essential nutrients sans the carbs.

For keto-vegans, the main goals are to consume a lot of plant-based fats, moderate amounts of plant-based proteins, and minimal carbs. To guide you, let's go through a list of foods that you can eat while following this diet. In the beginning, you may have to keep this list in your kitchen to serve as your reference. Over time, you will become more familiar with the kinds of foods you can eat, making it easier for you to follow the diet. Here is a quick look at the foods you can consume on the keto-vegan diet:

- Condiments and Sauces

Chili or hot sauce, mustard, hummus, salsa, soy sauce or tamari, vinegar, and tomato sauce.

- Fruits

Avocados, coconuts, blueberries, lemons, cranberries, olives, limes, strawberries, raspberries, watermelon, and tomatoes.

- Nuts and Seeds

Almonds, chia seeds, Brazil nuts, hemp seeds, hazelnuts or filberts, pumpkin seeds, macadamia nuts, sunflower seeds, pecans, pine nuts, peanuts, and walnuts.

- Nut Butters and Seed Butters

Almond butter, hazelnut butter, coconut butter or coconut manna, peanut butter, macadamia nut butter, sunflower seed butter, pecan butter, and tahini walnut butter.

- Healthy Oils

Almond oil, cacao butter, avocado oil, flaxseed oil, coconut oil, macadamia nut oil, hazelnut oil, olive oil, and MCT oil.

- Staple refrigerator items

Apple cider vinegar, cheese (dairy-free), yogurt (dairy-free), micro-greens, pickles, seitan, sauerkraut, tempeh, all types of sprouts, and tofu.

- Staple pantry items

Almond flour, baking powder, artichoke hearts, coconut flour, baking soda, cocoa or cacao powder, coconut milk (full fat), glucomannan powder, dark chocolate, jackfruit (canned), hearts of palm, nutritional yeast, psyllium husk, and vanilla extract (keto-vegan-friendly).

- Staple meal items

Herbs and spices, kelp noodles, edamame, lupini beans, kelp flakes, nori sheets, shirataki noodles, and roasted seaweed.

- Vegetables

Artichoke hearts, asparagus, arugula, beets, bell peppers, broccoli, bok choy, cabbage, Brussels sprouts, cauliflower, carrots, celeriac, celery, collard greens, chard, Daikon radishes, cucumbers, eggplant, dandelion greens, fennel, endive, garlic, fiddleheads, jicama, kohlrabi, kale, mushrooms, all types of lettuce, okra, mustard greens, radishes, onions, rutabaga, rhubarb, spinach, shallots, summer squash, winter squash, turnips, Swiss chard, and zucchini.

- Whole Foods

Avocados, olives, and coconuts.

As you can see, there are a lot of options for you to choose from. In terms of what you shouldn't eat while following the vegan-keto diet, these include:

- All types and forms of sugar

- Animal products like meat, poultry, fish, eggs, dairy, and more

- Gelatin

- Grains such as pasta, rice, wheat, and more

- High-carb nuts such as cashews, chestnuts, pistachios, and more

- Legumes

- Refined vegetable oils

- Starchy vegetables such as potatoes, yams, and more

- Trans fats or partially-hydrogenated oils

You can use all of the recommended keto-vegan food items as your ingredients for various dishes. To start you off, take a look at these simple, easy, and healthy recipes that fit right into your new lifestyle.

Keto Vegetable Soup

This soup is loaded with healthy veggies and other tasty ingredients that make it perfect for your new keto-vegan diet. It's simple, easy to make, and it will warm you up whenever the weather is cold.

Time: 45 minutes

Serving Size: 6 servings

Ingredients:

- ¾ tsp paprika
- 2 tsp Italian seasoning mix
- 1 tbsp olive oil
- 1 tbsp tomato paste
- 1 ¾ cups kidney beans (rinsed then drained)
- 1 ¾ cups tomatoes (diced)
- 2 cups cabbage (chopped)
- 2 cups cauliflower florets
- 4 cups vegetable broth (low-sodium)
- black pepper (freshly ground)
- kosher salt

- parsley (freshly chopped)

- 1 bell pepper (chopped)

- 1 medium-sized zucchini (chopped)

- 2 carrots (thinly sliced)

- 2 celery stalks (thinly sliced)

- 4 cloves of garlic (minced)

- 1 medium-sized onion (chopped)

Directions:

1. Set an Instant Pot to the "Sauté" setting, add the oil, garlic, and onion, and season with pepper and salt.

2. Stir occasionally to cook until the onion becomes soft. Add the tomato paste and continue stirring for about a minute.

3. Add the rest of the ingredients and stir well to combine.

4. Lock the Instant Pot, set it on high, and allow the

soup to cook for about 12 minutes.

5. Open the lid, stir the soup, and add more salt and pepper as needed.

6. Spoon the soup into a bowl and garnish with parsley before serving.

Spaghetti Squash with Tomato and Mushroom

This is a delicious recipe that puts a healthy new twist on pasta. After swearing off carbs as part of your keto diet, you can still continue eating pasta simply by changing some of the ingredients.

Time: 40 minutes

Serving Size: 4 servings

Ingredients:

- ¼ cup pine nuts (toasted)
- ⅓ cup shallots or onions (chopped)
- 1 cup mushrooms (sliced)
- 2 cups tomatoes (diced)

- a handful of basil (fresh, chopped)
- black pepper (freshly ground)
- kosher salt
- 2 spaghetti squash (cooked)
- 4 garlic cloves (minced)
- a pinch of red pepper flakes (optional)
- Parmesan cheese (optional)

Directions:

1. After cooking the spaghetti squash, allow to cool. Slice both pieces in half, remove all of the seeds, use a fork to shred, and set aside—this will be your noodles.

2. Heat oil in a sauté pan over medium heat. Add the mushrooms and onions, cook while stirring constantly for about 4 minutes. Add the garlic and continue stirring for 2 more minutes until fragrant.

3. Add the tomatoes while you continue

stirring. Then add the squash "noodles" and toss until all ingredients are evenly mixed.

4. Add the pine nuts and basil then continue tossing. Season with pepper, salt, and the optional seasonings before serving.

Roasted Veggie Masala

This veggie dish is spiced, healthy, and extremely flavorful. It's an excellent low-carb variation of the traditional Indian dish, making it perfect for your new diet.

Time: 30 minutes

Serving Size: 4 servings

Ingredients for the vegetables:

- 1 ¾ cups cauliflower florets
- ¾ cup green beans (sliced)
- ½ cup mushrooms (quartered)

Ingredients for the masala:

- ¼ tsp garam masala
- ¼ tsp turmeric
- ½ tsp chili (ground)
- 2 tbsp melted butter, ghee, or olive oil
- 2 tbsp ginger (fresh, minced)
- ½ cup tomato puree
- black pepper (freshly ground)
- kosher salt
- 1 clove of garlic (minced)

Ingredients for the garnish:

- cilantro (chopped)
- green onion (sliced)
- Sriracha

Directions:

1. Preheat your oven to 400°F and grease a sheet pan.

2. In a bowl, combine the tomato puree, ginger, garlic, other masala ingredients, and melted butter. Add the vegetables and toss to coat all the ingredients evenly.

3. Transfer the vegetables on the sheet pan, then season with pepper and salt.

4. Place the sheet pan in the oven and roast the vegetables for about 20 minutes. Garnish before serving.

Balsamic-Glazed Mushrooms

This is a tasty and healthy side dish that you can pair with your main meals. If you have a Slow Cooker, you can easily whip up this recipe and enjoy it however you want to.

Time: 2 hours and 15 minutes

Serving Size: 4 servings

Ingredients:

- ¼ tsp black pepper
- ½ tsp sea salt

- 1 tbsp tamari
- 2 tbsp balsamic vinegar
- 2 tbsp maple syrup
- ¼ cup olive oil
- 4 cups mushrooms (preferably baby portobello)
- 4 cloves of garlic (finely diced)

Directions:

1. Prepare the mushrooms by cutting off each of their tips. Then use a damp cloth to wipe them clean.
2. Combine all the ingredients in your Slow Cooker and stir well.
3. Set on high and cook for about 2 hours. You can cook the mushrooms for a longer time if you wish. Serve hot or allow to cool before serving.

Green Smoothie

If you're looking for the perfect recipe for a keto-vegan smoothie, look no further! This green smoothie will keep you energized and is chock full of superfood ingredients that will keep you focused and full throughout the day.

Time: 5 minutes

Serving Size: 1 smoothie

Ingredients:

- ½ tsp matcha powder
- 1 tsp vanilla extract (pure)
- 2 tsp MCT oil powder
- 1 tbsp keto-vegan sweetener
- ½ cup coconut milk
- ⅔ cup spinach
- ⅔ cup water
- ½ of a medium-sized avocado

- 5 ice cubes
- ½ tsp maca root powder (optional)
- ½ tsp turmeric (optional)
- ½ tbsp chia seeds (optional)
- 1 tbsp collagen powder (optional)
- ¼ cup protein powder (vanilla flavor, optional)

Directions:

1. Combine all of the ingredients—including the optional ingredients of your choice—in a blender.
2. Blend to combine well. Pour into a glass and enjoy!

Cauliflower and Zucchini Fritters

These easy-to-make fritters are crunchy, scrumptious, and totally meat-free. You can have them as a snack or as a light meal. Either way, you're sure to enjoy the unique texture and flavor combination.

Time: 10 minutes

Serving Size: 8 medium-sized fritters

Ingredients:

- ¼ tsp black pepper
- ½ tsp sea salt
- ¼ cup keto-appropriate flour
- 3 cups cauliflower (chopped)
- 2 medium-sized zucchini

Directions:

1. Use a food processor to grate the zucchini.

2. Steam or boil the cauliflower until fork-tender, about 5 minutes. Add the softened cauliflower to the food processor to break down into small pieces.

3. Place the grated veggies in a nut milk bag or a clean dish towel and squeeze tightly to remove the moisture.

4. Place the vegetables in a bowl. Add the rest of the ingredients and mix thoroughly to combine well.

5. Shape the mixture into medium-sized fritters and set aside.

6. Heat up coconut oil in a pan and cook the fritters for about 2 to 3 minutes on each side. Serve hot.

Portobello Mushrooms Stuffed with Curried Spinach

This is a "meaty" dish sans the meat that will fill you up and satisfy your taste buds. You can eat this dish as your main meal because of how substantial and healthy it is. And the best part is—it's so easy to make!

Time: 45 minutes

Serving Size: 4 servings

Ingredients for the stuffing:

- ½ tsp salt
- 2 tsp lemon zest

- 2 tsp yellow curry paste
- 1 ½ cups coconut milk
- 2 cups spinach (frozen)

Ingredients for the mushrooms:

- ¼ cup nuts (your choice)
- ¼ cup vinegar salad dressing and oil blend
- 4 big Portobello mushroom caps

Directions:

1. Allow the spinach to thaw before squeezing dry.
2. Heat up a pan on medium heat then add the yellow curry paste along with a couple of tablespoons of coconut milk. Stir while cooking until fragrant.
3. Add the rest of the coconut milk, lemon zest, and spinach. Season with salt. Stir well to combine and continue cooking until the mixture gets a creamy, thick consistency.

Set aside to cool.

4. Prepare the Portobello mushrooms by removing the stems and using a spoon to scrape out all of the gills.

5. Rub the salad dressing mixture on the surface of the mushroom caps then place them on a pan with the stem side up.

6. Place two teaspoons of the salad dressing mixture in each of the mushroom caps then spread well. Season with pepper and salt then cover and allow to marinate for one hour.

7. Heat your grill on high and place the mushroom caps with the stem down. Grill for 5 minutes, flip, and grill for another 5 minutes.

8. Spoon the spinach curry mixture into each of the mushroom caps, place in the oven and broil for around 3 to 5 minutes.

9. Sprinkle chopped nuts over the

mushrooms before serving.

Keto-Vegan Chili

Nothing can fill you up like a good bowl of chili. With this keto-vegan version, you can enjoy a high-protein, low-carb meal without feeling guilty!

Time: 40 minutes

Serving Size: 6 servings

Ingredients for the chili:

- 1 ½ tsp cinnamon (ground)
- 1 ½ tsp paprika (smoked)
- 2 tsp chili powder
- 4 tsp cumin (ground)
- 1 tbsp cocoa powder (unsweetened)
- 1 ½ tbsp tomato paste
- 2 tbsp olive oil
- ½ cup coconut milk

- 1 cup cremini mushrooms
- 1 cup walnuts (raw, minced)
- 1 ¾ cups tomatoes (finely diced)
- 2 ½ cups soy meat substitute (crumbled)
- 3 cups water
- black pepper (freshly ground)
- kosher salt
- 2 bell peppers (finely diced)
- 2 cloves of garlic (minced)
- 2 zucchini (finely diced)
- 5 celery stalks (finely diced)

Ingredients for serving:

- 2 tbsp cilantro leaves (fresh)
- 2 tbsp radishes (sliced)
- 1 medium-sized avocado (sliced)

Directions:

1. Heat up oil in a pot over medium heat. Add the diced celery then cook for about 4 minutes.

2. Add the cinnamon, cumin, garlic, paprika, and chili powder then stir for about 2 minutes until fragrant.

3. Add the mushrooms, bell peppers, and zucchini then continue cooking for 5 more minutes.

4. Reduce the heat and add the tomatoes, tomato paste, coconut milk, soy meat substitute, chipotle, cocoa powder, and walnuts. Simmer for 20 to 25 minutes until the vegetables soften and the mixture thickens.

5. Season with pepper and salt according to your taste.

6. Spoon the chili into bowls, top with the serving ingredients, and serve while hot.

Keto-Vegan Bibimbap

Asian dishes are always quite popular—and for good reason. If you're craving bibimbap, the famous Korean dish, then why don't you whip up this keto-vegan version. It's just as tasty, it's healthy, and it won't hinder you from reaching your diet goals.

Time: 25 minutes

Serving Size: 2 servings

Ingredients:

- 1 tsp sesame oil
- 1 tbsp soy sauce
- 2 tbsp gochujang chili paste
- 2 tbsp rice vinegar
- 2 tbsp sesame seeds
- ¾ cup tempeh (cubed)
- 1 ¼ cups cauliflower (raw, riced)
- ½ cucumber (sliced into strips)

- keto sweetener (concentrated liquid)
- 1 carrot (grated)
- 1 small bell pepper (sliced into strips)
- 5 broccoli florets (sliced thinly)

Directions:

1. Combine the vinegar and soy sauce in a bowl and mix well. Dip in the cubed tempeh and set aside to marinate.

2. Heat up oil in a skillet on medium heat and fry the marinated tempeh. After cooking, transfer the tempeh to a bowl.

3. Place the pan back on the heat and add the broccoli, carrots, and peppers. Cover the skillet with a lid and allow the veggies to cook for about two minutes.

4. In another pan, stir fry the riced cauliflower until tender. After cooking, take the skillet and the pan out of the heat.

5. In a bowl, combine the vinegar, oil, sweetener, and soy sauce then mix well.

6. Spoon the stir-fried cauliflower onto plates and top it off with the tempeh, cooked veggies, and raw cucumber.

7. Drizzle with sauce and sprinkle with sesame seeds before serving.

Tofu Scramble

This is a high-protein recipe that you can whip up in half an hour. It's the perfect breakfast to start your day and it's loaded with flavorful ingredients. Your family will surely love it as much as you.

Time: 30 minutes

Serving Size: 4 servings

Ingredients for the tofu scramble:

- 3 tbsp vegetable broth (low-sodium)
- ¾ cup mushrooms (sliced)
- 3 cups greens (your choice, roughly

chopped)

- ½ medium-sized onion (diced)
- 1 big bell pepper (diced)
- 1 block organic tofu (extra firm, pressed then drained)

Ingredients for the curry sauce:

- ¼ tsp coriander
- ¼ tsp garam masala
- ¼ tsp black or Himalayan pink salt
- ¼ tsp turmeric
- ¼ tsp paprika
- ½ tsp cumin
- ½ tsp garlic powder
- ½ tsp curry powder
- 1 tbsp water

Directions:

1. First, press the tofu to drain out all of its water content. Do this using a tofu press for a faster and more efficient process.

2. After pressing, break the tofu up into different-sized chunks.

3. In a bowl, combine all of the sauce ingredients and mix well. Add the sauce to the tofu and set aside to marinate.

4. In a pan, add the broth and sauté the onions for about 5 minutes. Add the red peppers and mushrooms then continue cooking for about 10 more minutes.

5. Add the marinated tofu and continue sautéing for 3 more minutes.

6. Add the chopped greens then cover your pan. Cook for about 5 minutes until the greens wilt. Serve hot.

Tofu and Roasted Cauliflower Tacos

These hearty tacos are loaded with tasty ingredients and they're super easy to make. One bite and you'll be hooked. These tacos are low-carb, ultra-satisfying, and will keep you feeling light but satisfied.

Time: 40 minutes

Serving Size: 8 tacos

Ingredients for the vegetables:

- 1 tsp chili powder
- 1 tsp cumin
- 1 tsp garlic powder
- 1 tsp onion powder
- 1 tsp paprika (smoked)
- 2 cups cremini mushrooms (sliced)
- black pepper (freshly ground)
- kosher salt
- olive oil
- 1 medium-sized cauliflower (remove the florets)

- 2 medium-sized bell peppers (sliced)

Ingredients for the crumbled tofu:

- ⅛ tsp black pepper
- ¼ tsp sea or Himalayan pink salt
- 1 tsp cumin
- 1 tsp paprika (smoked)
- 1 tbsp chili powder
- 1 tbsp olive oil
- 1 tbsp tomato paste
- 1 tbsp Worcestershire sauce (vegan)
- 1 block organic tofu (extra-firm, pressed then drained)
- 1 medium-sized red onion (diced)
- 3 cloves of garlic (minced)

Ingredients for wraps and toppings:

- 1 avocado (sliced)

- hot sauce

- lettuce leaves or low-carb tortillas

- mixed greens (arugula, butter lettuce, kale)

Directions:

1. First, press the tofu to drain out all of its water content. Do this using a tofu press for a faster and more efficient process. After pressing, crumble the tofu up.

2. Preheat your oven to 400°F and grease a baking sheet.

3. Arrange the vegetables on the tray in one layer. Drizzle olive oil over the veggies.

4. Add all the spices to the veggies and toss lightly until evenly coated.

5. Place the baking sheet in the oven and bake the veggies for about 30 minutes.

6. Heat up a skillet over medium heat and sauté the onion in olive oil for 10 minutes.

7. Add the Worcestershire sauce, tomato paste, and garlic then continue cooking for 2 more minutes.

8. Add the crumbled tofu to the skillet along with the paprika, chili powder, cumin, pepper, and salt. Mix all the ingredients together to combine well.

9. Reduce the heat and continue cooking for 10 more minutes while stirring occasionally.

10. Take the baking sheet out of the oven, the skillet out of the heat, and start building your tacos. Top them off with mixed greens, avocado, and hot sauce.

Mexican-Style Cauliflower Rice

You can enjoy this spicy "rice" as a side dish or as a component in a burrito. This is a keto-vegan recipe that incorporates authentic Mexican flavors.

Time: 15 minutes

Serving Size: 8 servings

Ingredients:

- 1 tbsp olive oil
- 2 tbsp serrano pepper (finely chopped)
- 2 tbsp tomato paste
- ½ cup onion (chopped)
- 8 cups cauliflower (cut roughly)
- black pepper (freshly ground)
- cilantro (chopped)
- kosher salt
- limes
- 2 cloves of garlic (minced)

Directions:

1. Use a food processor to rice the cauliflower.
2. Warm olive oil in a skillet over medium heat. Add the onion and cook until

translucent.

3. Add serrano pepper and garlic then cook for one more minute.

4. Add the riced cauliflower, pepper, salt, and tomato paste. Continue cooking until tender.

5. Serve hot with limes and cilantro.

Conclusion: Starting Your Keto-Vegan Journey

In this book, we started off with the ketogenic diet. If this is the first time you've learned about this diet, you now know what it is, how it works, the different types of keto diets you can follow, and the benefits of this diet. This information helps you determine how you can best start on the keto diet. Even if you have already started the keto diet and have been following it for some time now, this information serves as a refresher for you. Through this chapter, you would have been able to review everything you know about the keto diet—and you may have also learned something new!

The second chapter is all about the other half of the keto-vegan diet. For most vegans, they consider veganism a lifestyle instead of just a diet. This is especially true for those who have chosen to go vegan for ethical reasons. No matter what your reason is for going vegan, this chapter helped you understand veganism in greater detail. From what the diet is, what it means to be vegan, the benefits of going vegan, and how you can overcome the common challenges of veganism, this chapter includes a lot of information to guide you and help you determine how to become a true vegan.

Chapter three is where we put together these trendy diets to form a winning combination. This chapter is where you learned all about the keto-vegan diet—we discussed why both diets work so well together, the benefits you can enjoy from this diet combination, and some helpful tips and strategies for you to start and stick with this diet. As you have learned, the keto-vegan diet can help you achieve your health and weight-loss goals in fun, challenging, and interesting ways. Using the information in this chapter will help ensure your success as you embark on this new journey.

Speaking of ensuring your success, chapter four also contained a wealth of information. This chapter contained a comprehensive list of the recommended foods on the keto-vegan diet. In the beginning, you may want to make a copy of this list to keep in your kitchen. This will serve as your reference for when you're meal planning or when you need to make your weekly shopping list. Then we continued with ten healthy, easy, and tasty recipes that will make you celebrate the fact that you've chosen to become a keto-vegan.

As you can see, this book provided you with all the information you need about the keto-vegan diet—as promised. With this information, you don't have to worry about your health being an issue anymore. You can start your keto-vegan journey then use everything you've learned here to make it easier to follow this beneficial lifestyle. If there is one thing you should have taken away from this book—it is the knowledge that the keto-vegan diet is easy to follow as long as you know what it is, what you can eat on it, and how to follow it. With that being said... good luck on your new journey!

Super Easy Vegetarian Keto Cookbook

The proven way to lose weight healthily with the ketogenic diet, even if you're a clueless beginner

By: Amy Moore

Introduction

You now have in your hands a compendium of knowledge on getting started with a ketogenic or ketosis (keto) diet.

With this book, you have taken the first step towards creating a healthier and more active version of you, and it all starts with a low-fat, low-carb, high-protein keto diet. But first, a little bit about food. Yes, this part is important so hang tight.

Food is a source of fuel. Our body depends on food (and water) to get all the nutrients and nourishment we need to keep us functioning normally. Just like fuel, we should ensure that we are using the good stuff to make the engines of our body run smoothly.

At the same time, food can be something more than merely a source of nutrients. There is so much joy in having a delicious meal that oozes with flavor and character. You get a sense of joy when you dig into a delicious dessert or a lip-smacking starter. It is no wonder that many people around the world explore this planet solely to taste the different foods they can find. These so called "foodie-travelers" live to find out what flavors can be found in countries and locales around the world. They give us a glimpse of all the delicious dishes that they indulge in.

Which is why, when we think of worldly foods, we often think of exotic herbs, meat (all kinds of meat), and spices.

We never think about matching keto with anything exotic or flavorful. Keto is the bland stuff. Keto is for people who don't enjoy food.

A lot of people believe that a keto diet is boring, that there are no flavors to experiment with, and is typically boiled vegetables tossed around with a small helping of salt.

Well, they are wrong. The whole idea behind keto is not to sacrifice flavor. In fact, what you are doing is simply removing ingredients that are not good for you and adding more of the healthy stuff. That does not automatically imply that the food is drab and uninteresting. The reality is quite far from this assumption people make about keto.

So, we are going to take a journey. We are going to be the keto foodie-travelers, and our quest is to enjoy the entire process of keto with some delicious, healthy, and joyful food.

Welcome to the Super Easy Vegetarian Keto Cookbook. Let's begin.

Chapter 1: Keto is the New Hero

The keto diet has been in existence for a long time. Only recently has it been gaining in popularity, though. One of the main reasons is the fact that it is not just something health specialists and nutritionists recommend, but a diet that even doctors themselves have adopted. Don't believe me? Why not check out the YouTube page Doctor Mike, managed by Dr. Mikhail "Mike" Varshavski who has more than 4 million followers as of the writing of this book.

He has been talking about the keto diet for years and even tried it himself!

Before you think to yourself, "Boy, what scam are they selling me this time?" let me assure you that this is not a con or a scam. The keto diet works, and it has shown some incredible results to people who have adopted it.

But then, we haven't answered the important question yet.

What is a Keto Diet?

You see, the fundamental idea behind the diet is to activate your body's own fat-burning mechanisms. This is done as a source of fuel that the body might use for energy throughout the day. This means that the fat you consume, as well as the fat stored in your body, are all sources of fuel that your body can tap into!

The entire process of the keto diet is related to ketosis. That sounds like another fancy term, so what is it?

Essentially, ketosis is a state of the body. It is when the body produces molecules called ketones that are created by the liver. Ketones are created by the body to act as a source of energy to the cells and organs and can replace glucose as a source of fuel.

Our traditional diet consists of carbohydrates and, of course, sugar. Both of these substances produce the glucose required by the body. However, our body begins to depend on them a lot. Think of it like the body becoming addicted.

How can that happen?

When the body needs to use glucose, it requires the help of insulin, which is a type of hormone in our body. This hormone acts like a messenger and sends information to the cells to open up and allow the glucose to flow into them. The cells in turn send the glucose to the mitochondria, which are the energy generators in our cells.

The more sugar and carbs we consume, the more glucose we have in our cells. Doesn't that mean our body has more energy? Doesn't that imply we could run for 2 miles without breaking a sweat?

The body is a bit more complicated than that.

When the amount of sugar content in your blood increases, so does the insulin levels (to ensure that all the sugar content in your blood gets consumed). When the metabolic functions in the body are normal, then the cells easily accept the insulin produced by the body (these hormones are produced in the pancreas).

However, the metabolic functions do not always remain normal. You see, over time, the cells become resistant to the insulin because of just how much there is in the blood and how often it is produced. The pancreas then goes into panic mode. They need to make sure that the sugar in your blood is consumed. But what can it do?

It produces even more insulin to normalize the blood-sugar levels.

Let's try and see if we can understand the above using an analogy.

Say that you own a restaurant. All the patrons who visit your restaurant are cells, and the favorite dish on the menu is glucose. Lucky you! You have a lot of the stuff. However, you need something to serve all the glucose to your customers. Thankfully, you have your trusty staff of insulin to do the job. Eventually, you realize that you are getting too many orders for glucose, and you are unable to serve the customers. So you decide to bring in more insulin to work for you from the head office, also called the pancreas. Eventually, you realize that you have used all your insulin staff. Your pancreas have no more people to spare for your restaurant. So what do you do? You outsource the insulin from elsewhere.

This is essentially what happens in your body as well. Your pancreas eventually runs out of insulin, which can cause type 2 diabetes. Remember the part about outsourcing insulin for your restaurant? Well, that happens to your body. The only difference is that you are outsourcing insulin into your body in the form of insulin shots or medications.

Let me make something clear – insulin and glucose are not our body's enemies. In fact, do you know the major source of energy for your brain? Why, it's glucose of course! Simply put, you should not cut off glucose from your body.

The problem lies with our consumption of glucose. In today's world, we are spoilt for choice when it comes to fat-induced, sugar-heavy, and carbohydrate-rich food. The idea that more is better is prevalent in our society. Many food outlets and restaurants are focused on adding as much as possible in their dishes, from extra cheesy fries with extra Doritos to that ice-cream churros cookie dessert with chocolate sauce and two layers of extra-sweet waffles.

Wherever you turn, you can find fat, sugar, and carbs waiting for you. While their offers are always tempting, we are going to resist their influence.

Why Choose a Keto Diet?

There are many reasons why one chooses a keto diet. To many, it is the change in lifestyle. They want to switch from a diet that does not give them the right fuel. To others, they want a diet that compliments their workout or exercise routines. While many others want a diet to help them lose weight.

All these goals can be achieved through a keto diet.

Let's take a step back through history. During the time of our ancestors, when they were hunter-gatherers, agriculture wasn't that popular, and the food you consumed depended on what you gathered or killed.

This led to a particular scenario where there might be no food for days at a time. The body had to find ways to keep its human host alive. So when glucose would enter our bodies, insulin would be dispatched to carry it into our organs as well as hoard the unused glucose into fat cells for future use.

This helped our ancestors automatically enter into a state of ketosis; though, our ancestors never knew that. Their bodies would use the stored fats as energy. The result, our ancestors had leaner and healthier bodies since we evolved to consume these fats properly into the body.

Fast forward to the present times. There is no shortage of restaurants, street stalls, and fast-food chains to tempt you into getting something. In fact, convenience is part of lives to such an extent that we can get most of what we want through the touch of a few buttons.

Rather than give our body necessary fats, we are pumping it with more carbs.

Wait, did you just read the fact that we have to give our body more fats? Isn't the point of keto reducing weight?

Before you start wondering whether keto is truly effective or not, let me explain.

There are so many misconceptions about fats. With the way that people around the world treat the concept of fats, it is as though any fat is harmful to our body.

The reality is that we need a certain amount of fats. In fact, we need the good fats. One good group of fats are monounsaturated fats. You can find these in your body in a liquid state when your body is at room temperature. However, they can become more solid when you are in colder or cooler temperatures. These days, you are not going to find any medical professional who has anything negative to say about monounsaturated fats. In fact, they are actually considered good for the heart.

Now, where do we get this good fat?

We can eat foods like avocados, olive oil, many types of nuts, and a host of other ingredients that we will use in the dishes we prepare.

But good fat is not the only thing that we will be consuming. In addition to fats, we are going to make sure we receive the right amount of proteins as well.

All the Wonderful Benefits of Keto Diet

Apart from preventing type 2 diabetes, there are more benefits to keto than you might have originally thought. Let's look at some of them.

Aids in weight loss

Need to lose weight effectively? No problem! With the combination of a keto diet and regular workout routine, you will be shedding weight much better than most techniques. Additionally, once you get used to the diet, you don't feel hungry easily, and the protein-rich food you have aids you in your exercises.

Reduces the risk of diabetes

We saw how diabetes is caused in our body. With a proper keto diet, you are reducing the risk of the disease from occurring. You are giving your body essential nutrients and reducing the amount of glucose you ingest.

Improves heart health

When you are on a keto diet, you are also reducing the intake of harmful cholesterol. This eventually improves the functioning of your heart. In fact, your body's good cholesterol, HDL, increases while the levels of bad cholesterol, known as LDL, decreases.

Improves brain functioning

Many studies have been conducted on ketosis. One such study claims that keto improves brain function (Hernandez et al., 2018). More specifically, it improves cognitive functioning and alertness.

Reduces fat molecules

There are certain fat molecules that circulate in your bloodstream known as triglycerides. These molecules are well known for being a risk factor for heart diseases.

One of the main causes for the increase in triglycerides is the consumption of carbs. This is why, when people reduce their intake of carbs and switch to healthier foods, they begin to notice a decrease in the circulation of triglycerides.

The Bottom Line

A keto diet is more than just a fad. It is a lifestyle sprinkled with benefits. We are going to take full advantage of that. Still with me here? Then, let's head out to our next destination – all the food you can eat and the ones you should generally avoid.

Chapter 2: What to Eat and What Not to Eat

This is an important question and many times, we might often find ourselves feeling lost with different opinions on what exactly should constitute a keto diet.

Thankfully, you have this book.

I am going to list the foods that you can include as part of your keto diet and those foods that you should definitely avoid. First, we will focus on percentages.

When we break down your typical keto diet into its macronutrients, your intake should look like this:

- 75% fats
- 20% proteins
- 5% carbohydrates

Usually, our daily intake of calories should be around 2,000. Which means that if we apply the percentages, fats should provide us with around 1,500 calories, proteins should contribute 400 calories, and carbs should give us the remaining 100 calories.

So, you should be aiming to hit your daily fat requirement, thinking about how much protein you are having, and limiting your carb intake. Then, we will remove any meat products from the list (after all, we are focused on the awesome veggie stuff). Even still, there are numerous foods that you can enjoy on a keto diet.

Since we mentioned the good fats, let's start by looking at the ways you can get some healthy fats in your body.

Healthy fats

Make sure that you avoid trans fats. Bearing that in mind, here are some sources of polyunsaturated and monounsaturated fats:

- Butter
- Coconut oil
- Ghee
- Lard
- Avocado oil
- Extra virgin olive oil
- Macadamia oil
- Coconut butter
- Coconut milk

We are going to have a well-rounded understanding of what foods you can definitely enjoy on a keto diet, the foods that you should keep in moderation, and those foods that are a definite no-no. In short, we are looking at "The Good, The Moderate, and The Bad" foods.

With that established, let's find out about the...

Foods You Can Enjoy on the Keto Diet

When you include vegetables, then you are adding in as many essential nutrients into your diet as possible while reducing calories, which helps you remain within your daily intake goals.

Vegetables

- Artichokes
- Asparagus
- Avocado
- Bell peppers
- Broccoli
- Cabbage
- Cauliflower
- Celery
- Cucumber
- Kohlrabi
- Lettuce
- Okra or ladies' fingers
- Radishes

- Seaweed
- Spinach
- Tomatoes
- Watercress
- Zucchini

Dairy products

Most people often hesitate when it comes to dairy products because they are often left wondering just what to include and what they should not consume. To put your mind at ease, here are the products that you can definitely include into your diet:

- Brie cheese
- Cottage cheese
- Cheddar cheese
- Cream cheese
- Full-fat yogurt
- Heavy cream
- Kefir
- Mozzarella cheese
- Sour cream

- Swiss cheese

You see? You are still going to enjoy some really mouth-watering food!

Herbs and spices

You have a wide selection of herbs and spices that you can add into your dish. Plus, you are not adding a high amount of carbs or calories into your food, while at the same time, you have incredible flavors to work with. Herbs and spices that you can work with are:

- Basil
- Black pepper
- Cayenne
- Cardamom
- Chili powder
- Cilantro
- Cinnamon
- Cumin
- Curry powder
- Garam masala
- Ginger

- Garlic
- Nutmeg
- Oregano
- Onion powder
- Paprika
- Parsley
- Rosemary
- Sea salt
- Sage
- Thyme
- Turmeric
- White pepper

Beverages

No sweet stuff on the keto diet, of course. That does not mean that you are prohibited from enjoying any flavored beverage. You can still indulge in certain beverages to provide you with a little variety when you feel like having something other than plain water.

- Almond milk unsweetened
- Cashew milk unsweetened

- Club soda
- Coconut milk
- Coffee
- Herbal tea
- Mineral water
- Seltzer water
- Tea

Now that we have a grasp of the good stuff that you can enjoy, let's move on to those foods that you can have in moderation. But what does moderation mean?

In other words, when you are able to get your carbs under control and when you are used to the keto diet, you can make adjustments wherever necessary to enjoy the below foods. This way, you keep your calorie intake within the limit, but at the same time, you can enjoy something you want.

Fruits

There's no doubt about it – fruits are a wonderful source of nutrition. But they also include sugar, and that means we need to be careful about how much and, more importantly, which fruit we consume.

There are some fruits that have low to moderate amount of carbs. You can enjoy these fruits (in limited quantities).

Many of the fruits listed below can be enjoyed on a daily basis, but you might be limited to a cup or a single slice.

Surprised? Did you think I was going to say that you can only have them once a week?

Remember that as you get a better understanding of your calorie and carb intake, you can make adjustments to include more of the fruits below:

- Apricot
- Blackberries
- Blueberries
- Cantaloupe
- Cherries
- Cranberries
- Grapefruit
- Honeydew
- Kiwi
- Lemon
- Lime
- Peaches
- Raspberries

- Strawberries

Nuts and seeds

Nuts are a great source of healthy fats. At the same time, they also contain carbohydrates. Not to worry. They do not have the quantities of carbs that should worry you, and we are going to make sure that you have the right amount.

So what nuts can you have?

- Almonds
- Cashews
- Chia seeds
- Hazelnuts
- Macadamia nuts
- Nut butter
- Pecans
- Pine nuts
- Pistachios
- Psyllium
- Pumpkin seeds
- Sesame seeds

- Sunflower seeds
- Walnuts

With all the keto-approved foods that you can have in moderate amounts listed, we are going to look at all the foods you can't include in your diet.

All the Stuff That's a No-Go

There are numerous categories that you should avoid when you are on a keto diet. You might have heard this one, but it is important to mention it anyways – do not include any food that is a grain or based on grain, as they have a high amount of carbohydrates.

Some of the foods to avoid while on the keto diet are:

- Agave
- All-purpose flour
- Baked goods
- Baking mix
- Bananas
- Barley
- Beer
- Brown sugar
- Buckwheat

- Cake flour
- Candy
- Canola oil
- Cereal
- Corn
- Corn syrup
- Couscous
- Honey
- Hydrogenated oils
- Ice cream
- Juice cocktail
- Low-fat dairy
- Mangos
- Maple syrup
- Margarine
- Milk
- Milk chocolate

- Muesli
- Oats
- Pastry flour
- Pasta
- Pineapple
- Potatoes
- Quinoa
- Rice
- Snack bars
- Soda
- Sweet potatoes
- Sports drinks
- Wheat flour
- White sugar

That's all there is to it. When you look at the list above, you might be thinking if there is any way you can add of one those items as part of the keto diet. Perhaps once in a while won't hurt right?

However, we are going to focus solely on the foods that we can include and not even remotely consider any of the items in the list above. It is not going to be easy, but it is necessary. Once your body begins to understand that it should not depend on carbs or sugars anymore, it is much easier for it to adjust to the keto diet.

Now that we have established the basic guidelines on what you can eat or not eat, let's continue our journey. This time, we are heading straight for our most exciting destination – food!

We begin our adventure in the land of breakfast, the meal that literally means what its name indicates – to break the fast that you have been having overnight since your last meal (dinner if you are following the keto diet, which also means you are bidding farewell to those late night snacks).

Chapter 3: Delicious Breakfast Recipes

Breakfast, the meal that decides just how your day might be. With the right amount of nutrients, you can start your day feeling fresh with bountiful positive energy. If not, you might just feel like you are dragging your body around, with lethargy setting in and your brain thinking about heading back to bed.

Soft Keto Cream Cheese Pancakes

Didn't I tell you this was going to be fun? Yes, indeed. We are starting our day off with soft and cheesy pancakes that will make you want more.

Ingredients

- ½ teaspoon cinnamon
- ½ packet of Stevia in the Raw (a keto alternative to sugar)
- 1 tablespoon coconut flour
- 1 tablespoon coconut oil
- 3 tablespoons sugar-free maple syrup
- 2 oz. cream cheese
- 2 eggs

Directions

1. Take out a bowl and mix all the ingredients together, except the coconut oil, until they are smooth.

2. Next, take out a skillet or a non-stick pan and place it on medium-high heat.

3. Add in the coconut oil.

4. Now add the mixture into the pan and prepare your pancakes normally. The trick is to try and cook as much as possible on one side without burning it. To do this, simply use a spatula to lift up the side that is cooking to see if it has been cooked thoroughly.

5. When one side is to your liking, you can flip over the pancake and cook the other side.

6. When both sides are cooked, transfer the pancake over to a plate and enjoy!

Keto Spice Latte Boost

Why head over to your local cafe when you can make your very own healthy latte at home? Oh, did I mention it includes pumpkin spice?

Ingredients

- 10 drops liquid stevia
- 2 tablespoons heavy whipping cream
- 2 tablespoons butter

- 2 teaspoons pumpkin pie spice blend

- 2 cups strong coffee

- 1 cup coconut milk

- 1 teaspoon vanilla extract

- ½ teaspoon cinnamon

- ¼ cup pumpkin puree

Directions

1. Place a non-stick pan over medium heat.

2. Add in the pumpkin puree, butter, milk, and the spice blend.

3. Allow them to reach boiling point, and once you notice that they are bubbling, add in the 2 cups of coffee into the mixture. Stir the ingredients and mix them all together. Do this for about 2-3 minutes.

4. Once the ingredients are all mixed together, transfer them to a blender, add the stevia and cream. Blend all the ingredients together until they are smooth.

5. Transfer to your favorite coffee mug or coffee flask (that you can take to work).

Smooth Avocado and Kale Smoothie

What do you get when you add in two healthy and delicious ingredients to make a smoothie? Well, you get a deliciously healthy smoothie of course!

Ingredients

- 3 ice cubes
- 1 cup fresh kale (chopped)
- 1 tablespoon fresh lemon juice
- ½ teaspoon liquid stevia extract, to taste
- ¾ cup unsweetened almond milk
- ½ cup chopped avocado
- ¼ cup full-fat yogurt, plain

Directions

1. Combine the almond milk, kale, and avocado into a blender. Run the blender until the ingredients are smooth.
2. Add the remaining ingredients and blend again.
3. Transfer the ingredients into a large glass and drink immediately.

Almond Butter Protein Smoothie

Heading out to the gym? Why not have this drink to give you that boost of energy that you need? Or could even enjoy it on its own while getting ready for your day.

Ingredients

- 1 cup unsweetened almond milk

- 1 tablespoon almond butter

- ½ cup full-fat yogurt, plain

- ¼ cup vanilla egg white protein powder

- ¼ teaspoon ground cinnamon

- ¼ liquid stevia

Directions

1. Combine the almond milk and butter in a blender. Let the blender run until you see that the entire mixture is smooth.

2. Add the remaining ingredients and blend again.

3. Transfer the ingredients into a large glass and drink immediately.

Blueberry and Beets Smoothie

What do you get when you add in two healthy and delicious ingredients to make a smoothie? Well, you get a healthy and delicious smoothie of course!

Ingredients

- 1 cup unsweetened coconut milk
- 1 teaspoon chia seeds
- 1 small beet (peeled and chopped)
- ¼ cup heavy cream
- ¼ cup frozen blueberries
- ¼ liquid stevia

Directions

1. Combine coconut milk, beets, and blueberries into a blender. Run the blender until the ingredients are smooth.
2. Add the remaining ingredients and blend again.
3. Transfer the ingredients into a large glass and drink immediately.

Almond Muffins with Butter

Crunchy and delicious. The butter adds the right amount of texture to the whole dish. When you want your mornings to start off smoothly, then these muffins can help you with that.

Ingredients

- 4 large eggs
- 2 teaspoons baking powder

- 2 cups almond flour
- 1 cup powdered erythritol
- ¾ cup almond butter (warmed)
- ¾ cup unsweetened almond milk
- ¼ teaspoon salt

Directions

1. Preheat the oven to 350°F.

2. Take out a muffin pan and line it with paper liners.

3. Take a large bowl and add in the flour, erythritol, salt, and baking powder. Using a whisk, mix them properly.

4. Use another bowl and add the eggs, almond butter, and almond milk.

5. Now transfer the ingredients from the second bowl into the first. Mix all the ingredients together.

6. Using a spoon, transfer the batter that you have now into the muffin pan.

7. Transfer the pan into the oven and bake for about 20-25 minutes. To check if the muffins are ready, take a knife and insert it into the center of any muffin. When you remove it, there should not be much of the muffin sticking to it.

8. Allow the muffins to cool at room temperature for

about 5 minutes before you serve them.

Classic Omelet, Keto Style!

Sometimes, all you need is a nice omelet to make your day. But you don't want to have just any omelet. What you need is the keto brand of omelets. Like the one below.

Ingredients

- 3 large eggs (whisked)
- 2 teaspoons coconut oil
- 1 tablespoon heavy cream
- ¼ cup diced green pepper
- ¼ cup diced yellow onion
- ¼ teaspoon salt
- ¼ teaspoon pepper

Directions

1. Take out a small bowl and add in eggs, heavy cream, salt, and pepper. Whisk them together until they have mixed properly.

2. Place a skillet over medium heat and add in 1 teaspoon of coconut oil.

3. Add in the peppers and onions into the skillet and sauté for 3-4 minutes.

4. Transfer the mixture in the skillet into a bowl. Reheat the skillet on medium heat and add the remaining tablespoon of oil.

5. Take the bowl containing the whisked eggs and heavy cream and pour it into the skillet.

6. Cook until you notice the bottom of the eggs starting to set.

7. Here's a trick to getting the eggs right. Tilt the pan slightly to spread the egg and continue to cook until you see that they are almost set.

8. Take the bowl containing the peppers and onions. Using a spoon, spread them over half the egg. Fold it over.

9. Now, just wait for the eggs to cook completely before serving.

Protein Pancakes with a Cinnamon Twist

How about getting the right amount of proteins? How about doing it while having a pancake? How about adding cinnamon to the mix? All good questions that have only one answer, the recipe below.

Ingredients

- 8 large eggs

- 2 scoops egg white protein powder

- 1 cup canned coconut milk

- 1 teaspoon vanilla extract
- ¼ cup coconut oil
- ½ teaspoon ground cinnamon
- ½ teaspoon liquid stevia
- ¼ teaspoon ground nutmeg

Directions

1. Take out your food processor and add coconut milk, coconut oil, and eggs into it. Blend the ingredients together until they have been mixed well.

2. Add the remaining ingredients into the blender and continue to blend until you notice the mixture turn smooth.

3. Place a non-stick skillet over medium heat.

4. Add the batter you just prepared in the food processor into the skillet. Do not pour all of it in one go. Use a cup and pour ¼ of the batter for each pancake you would like to make.

5. Cook the batter until you notice bubbles forming on the top of the pancake and then flip it.

6. Cook the pancake until the underside turns brown.

7. Transfer to a plate and move on to the next pancake.

Green Smoothie for Detoxifying

Time to go green in the morning! This smoothie is filled with all the green goodness you can ask for. It's got kale, spinach, and celery. Add a bit of lemon juice and you have that incredible zest to compliment the drink.

Ingredients

- 3 ice cubes
- 2 tablespoons fresh lemon juice
- 1 cup fresh chopped kale
- 1 cup water
- 1 tablespoon coconut oil
- 1 tablespoon fresh lime juice
- ½ cup fresh baby spinach
- ¼ cup sliced celery
- ½ teaspoon liquid stevia extract

Directions

1. Combine kale, spinach, and celery into a blender. Run the blender until the ingredients are smooth.

2. Add the remaining ingredients and blend again.

3. Transfer the ingredients into a large glass and drink immediately.

Egg Muffins with Tomato and Mozzarella

Time to try a savoury version of a muffin. The tomato adds in the right amount of sweetness while the mozarella gives the tart flavor to add balance to the entire muffin. Don't take my word for it. Try it out yourself!

Ingredients

- 12 large eggs (whisked)
- 1 tablespoon butter
- 1 medium tomato (diced)
- 1 cup mozzarella cheese (shredded)
- ½ cup yellow onion (diced)
- ½ cup canned coconut milk
- ¼ cup sliced green onion
- ¼ teaspoon salt
- ¼ teaspoon pepper

Directions

1. Preheat the oven to about 350°F.
2. Take out a muffin tray and use a cooking spray to lightly grease it.
3. Take out a skillet and place over medium heat. Add the onions and tomatoes. Cook for about 3-4 minutes until

the ingredients soften.

4. Transfer the mixture into the muffin cups, making sure that you divide them equally.

5. Whisk together the coconut milk, eggs, green onions, salt, and pepper well in a small bowl. Transfer them equally into the muffin cups. The best way to do this is by using a spoon.

6. Add the cheese on top, pop the tray into the oven, and bake for about 20-25 minutes.

Crispy Chai Waffles

Love the magical flavor of chai? Well, how about transferring those flavors into a waffle. It's east meets west in this easy-to-make and delicious breakfast.

Ingredients

- 4 large eggs (separated into yolks and whites)
- 3 tablespoons coconut oil (melted)
- 3 tablespoons powdered erythritol
- 3 tablespoons unsweetened almond milk
- 3 tablespoons coconut flour
- 1 teaspoon baking powder
- 1 teaspoon vanilla extract
- ½ teaspoon ground cinnamon

- ¼ teaspoon ground ginger
- ¼ teaspoon ground cloves
- ¼ teaspoon ground cardamom

Directions

1. Take the egg whites and place them in one bowl while the yellows go into another bowl.

2. Start with the egg whites, whipping them until you notice peaks appear on them. Set aside the bowl for now.

3. Move on to the egg yolk. Add the coconut flour, erythritol, baking powder, vanilla, cinnamon, cardamom, and cloves into it and whisk all the ingredients together until they are mixed properly.

4. Add the coconut oil into the bowl with the yolk and continue whisking. Next, add in the almond milk and keep the whisk going!

5. Time to add in the egg whites. Fold them into the yolk and make sure that the ingredients are mixed in properly.

6. Take out the waffle iron and lightly grease it with cooking spray.

7. For the waffle, pour about ½ cup batter into the iron.

8. Prepare the waffle based on the instructions provided

to you by the iron manufacturer.

9. Once the waffle is prepared, transfer it to a plate and work on the remaining batter.

Protein Smoothie with Creamy Chocolate

With the power of the protein and the wonderful texture of the creamy chocolate, you might just make this your preferred protein smoothie. That is, if you are not left wondering which of the other smoothies in this book could be your favorite.

Ingredients

- 1 cup unsweetened almond milk
- 1 tablespoon unsweetened cocoa powder
- 1 tablespoon coconut oil
- ½ cup full-fat yogurt
- ¼ teaspoon liquid stevia
- ¼ cup chocolate egg white protein powder

Directions

1. Combine almond milk, yogurt, and protein powder into a blender. Run the blender until the ingredients are smooth.

2. Add the remaining ingredients and blend again.

3. Transfer the ingredients into a large glass and drink immediately.

Vanilla and Chai Smoothie Combo

A bit of the chai goodness with the kick of the vanilla. It's like bringing together peanut butter and jelly, only much healthier and more delightful.

Ingredients

- 1 cup unsweetened almond milk
- 1 teaspoon vanilla extract
- ½ cup full-fat yogurt
- ¼ teaspoon liquid stevia
- ¼ teaspoon ground cinnamon
- ¼ teaspoon ground ginger
- ¼ teaspoon ground cloves
- ¼ teaspoon ground cardamom

Directions

1. Combine all the ingredients into a blender. Run the blender until the ingredients are smooth.

2. Transfer the ingredients into a large glass and drink immediately.

Protein Pancakes with Chocolate

Consuming protein does not have to be boring. Now, you get your protein in a pancake with some chocolate.

Ingredients

- 8 large eggs
- 2 scoops egg white protein powder
- 1 teaspoon vanilla extract
- 1 cup canned coconut milk
- ¼ cup coconut oil
- ¼ cup unsweetened cocoa powder
- ¼ teaspoon liquid stevia extract

Directions

1. Take out the food processor and add the coconut milk, coconut oil, and eggs into it.

2. Blend in the ingredients using a few pulses. Add in the remaining ingredients.

3. Continue blending until all the ingredients have turned smooth.

4. Add in the stevia for flavor.

5. Now place a skillet over medium heat.

6. Time to work on the batter. Use ¼ cup of batter for each package that you make.

7. Begin cooking the pancake until you see bubbles form on top. Once you spot the bubbles, flip over the

pancake and continue cooking until a brown layer forms at the bottom.

8. Transfer to a plate and then use the remaining batter if you like.

Scrambled Eggs with Spinach and Parmesan

These eggs need just the right garnishments to turn them into something special. The spinach does not add in heavy flavors, but the nutty taste of parmesan is a wonderful compliment to both the eggs and spinach.

Ingredients

- 2 cups fresh baby spinach
- 2 tablespoons grated parmesan cheese
- 2 large eggs (whisked)
- 1 tablespoon heavy cream
- ¼ teaspoon salt
- ¼ teaspoon pepper
- 1 teaspoon coconut oil

Directions

1. Take a bowl and add in the whisked eggs. Add the heavy cream, salt, and pepper in it and whisk again until all ingredients are combined.

2. Place a skillet over medium heat and pour the coconut

oil into it.

3. Put the spinach into the skillet and cook until it wilts. This usually takes about 2 minutes.

4. Pour the ingredients from the bowl into the skillet and cook until you see the eggs set. This takes another 1-2 minutes.

5. Add the parmesan.

6. Serve hot.

Cinnamon Waffles

Another waffle option for you. This time, we are bringing in the spicy power of cinnamon with the right amount to vanilla extract to compliment the spice.

Ingredients

- 4 large eggs (separated into yolks and whites)
- 3 tablespoons coconut flour
- 3 tablespoons powdered erythritol
- 1 teaspoon baking powder
- 1 teaspoon vanilla extract
- ½ cup heavy cream
- ½ teaspoon ground cinnamon
- ¼ teaspoon ground nutmeg

Directions

1. Take the egg whites and place them in one bowl while the yellows go into another bowl.

2. Start with the egg whites, whipping them until you notice peaks appear on them. Set aside the bowl for now.

3. Move on to the egg yolk. Add in the coconut flour, erythritol, baking powder, vanilla, cinnamon, and nutmeg and whisk them all until they have blended together well. Add in the heavy cream and whisk again until the mixture has combined.

4. Finally, transfer the egg whites into the bowl and continue mixing everything.

5. Use your cooking spray to coat the waffle iron and preheat it.

6. Use ½ cup of batter for each waffle you would like to make.

7. Prepare the waffle based on the instructions of the waffle iron.

8. Once the waffle is ready, transfer it to a plate. Use the remaining batter if you like.

Pumpin' Pumpkin Spice Waffles

It's not just the pumpkin puree that brings out the flavor in this dish, but the combination of cloves, nutmeg, and cinnamon. This waffle is a spice fest, and you are invited to try it out (and get hooked on to the dish).

Ingredients

- 4 large eggs (separated into yolks and whites)
- 3 tablespoons powdered erythritol
- 3 tablespoons coconut flour
- 1 teaspoon vanilla extract
- 1 teaspoon baking powder
- ½ cup pumpkin puree
- ½ teaspoon ground cinnamon
- ¼ teaspoon ground nutmeg
- ¼ teaspoon ground cloves

Directions

1. Take the egg whites and place them in one bowl while the yellows go into another bowl.

2. Start with the egg whites, whipping them until you notice peaks appear on them. Set aside the bowl for now.

3. Move on to the egg yolk. Add in the coconut flour, erythritol, baking powder, vanilla, cinnamon, nutmeg, and cloves and whisk all the ingredients well.

4. Add in the pumpkin puree and continue whisking. Transfer the egg whites into the yolk and whisk a little more.

5. Use your cooking spray to coat the waffle iron and preheat it.

6. Use ½ cup of batter for each waffle you would like to make.

7. Prepare the waffle based on the instructions of the iron.

8. Once the waffle is ready, transfer it to a plate. Use the remaining batter if you like.

Keto Tea

A nice cup of tea in the morning? Perhaps to go along with your waffle or pancake? Of course. We even have a keto version.

Ingredients

- 2 cups water
- 2 tea bags
- 1 tablespoon ghee
- 1 tablespoon coconut oil
- ½ teaspoon vanilla extract
- ¼ teaspoon liquid stevia extract

Directions

1. Prepare your tea using the tea bags and then set it aside.

2. Take a different container and melt the ghee.

3. Add coconut oil and vanilla to the melted ghee.

4. Pour tea from mug into a blender. Add in the remaining ingredients.

5. Blend them until smooth.

Keto Oatmeal Cinnamon Spice

Sometimes, you just need a good ol' oatmeal to start your day. But no way are you going to resort to the same old stuff. It is time to spice it up a bit!

Ingredients

- 10 drops liquid stevia
- 3 tablespoons Erythritol (powdered)
- 3 tablespoons butter
- 3 cups coconut milk
- 2 cups cream cheese
- 1 teaspoon cinnamon
- 1 teaspoon unsweetened maple syrup
- 1 cup crushed pecans

- ½ teaspoon vanilla
- ½ cup cauliflower florets
- ¼ cup flax seed
- ¼ teaspoon allspice
- ¼ teaspoon nutmeg
- ¼ cup heavy cream
- ¼ cup chia seed

Directions

1. Add the cauliflower florets into the food processor and blend them well.

2. Take a pan and place it over medium heat. Add in the coconut milk.

3. In another pan, add in the crushed pecans and cook over low heat to toast.

4. Add the cauliflower to coconut milk and heat the mixture until it starts to boil. When you see it boiling, bring down the heat to simmer.

5. Add in all the spices into the coconut milk and mix the ingredients together.

6. Add the Erythritol, stevia, flax, and chia seeds into the coconut milk and mix them all together.

7. Combine cream, butter, and cream cheese to the pan and mix again.

8. Transfer to a bowl.

Keto Mexican Breakfast Fiesta

Hola and welcome to the dish that will bring in some mexican flavors, all while being keto! Think it impossible? Well, we made possible!

Ingredients

- 4 eggs (poached)
- 2 tablespoons sour cream
- 2 tablespoons olives (chopped)
- 2 tablespoons cilantro (chopped)
- ¼ cup chunky salsa
- ¼ cup cheddar cheese (shredded)
- ¼ cup avocado (chopped into chunks)

Directions

1. Prepare the eggs by poaching them.

2. Next, take a bowl that is microwave safe and add in the salsa. Heat it inside the microwave (which should take around 30-45 seconds).

3. Transfer the poached eggs onto a plate and then top it

with salsa, sour cream, olives, cheese, avocado, and parsley.

Shufflin' Breakfast Souffle

This souffle is so soft that you cannot help making a little shuffle after you are done eating it.

Ingredients

- 3 tablespoons unsalted butter
- ½ cup egg whites
- ½ cup thinly sliced mushrooms
- ½ cup fresh goat cheese
- ½ medium tomato (thinly sliced)
- ¼ teaspoon salt
- ¼ teaspoon pepper

Directions

1. Start by preheating the oven to 400°F.

2. Take out a bowl and combine the eggs, salt, and pepper and whip them together.

3. Place a skillet over medium to high heat. Toss in the butter into the pan and wait for it to melt. Add the mushrooms and sauté them until they are soft.

4. The tomato slices go into the pan next. Stir the

ingredients a little.

5. Add the cheese into the bowl with the egg whites. Fold them with the whites.

6. Pour the egg white mixture into the skillet.

7. Transfer everything over to the pan and bake for about 8 minutes.

8. Transfer to a plate and enjoy!

Cauliflower Hash Browns

We couldn't complete the breakfast section without having a hash brown recipe thrown in. The best part is that if you need to prepare a quick breakfast, then this is your recipe.

Ingredients

- 2 cups cauliflower florets
- 1 cup gluten-free flour
- 1 onion (chopped)
- 2 tablespoons butter (more if necessary)
- ¼ teaspoon salt
- ¼ teaspoon pepper

Directions

1. In a small bowl, add in the flour, cauliflower, onion, salt, and pepper and mix them well.

2. Take out a skillet and place it on medium heat.

3. Add the tablespoons of butter.

4. Take out the cauliflower and flour mixture in a scoop and roll it into a ball. Do not worry if the mixture does not stick together. It will once it has been transferred into the pan. Press on the ball with a spoon until it gains a disk shape.

5. Allow one side to fry and turn a nice brown color. This usually takes about 3-4 minutes. When one side is done, flip it over and work on the other side.

6. Transfer the hash brown over to a plate. Use the remaining flour mixture for more hash browns. Add more butter if required.

Chapter 4: Scrumptious Lunch Dishes

The afternoons are for taking a break from your heavy schedule or relaxing at home.

The best way to do any of that is by having a healthy and mouth-watering lunch dish right next you, where each bite bursts open with flavors. Welcome to the next step of our journey, where your taste buds will dance, explore, and experience dishes that you might never think could be possible with just vegetarian ingredients.

Well, they are.

Vegetarian Taco Salad with Avocado Lime Dressing

Another Mexican specialty, and we're going to make it keto style. So let's get started!

Ingredients for the Salad

- 15 ounces black beans (drained and rinsed)
- 4 ounces spring mix (or a mix of your favorite greens)
- 3 stalks green onion (chopped)
- 2 roma tomatoes (chopped)
- 2 tablespoons cilantro (freshly snipped)
- 2 ears of corn (cooked & corn removed)

- 1 avocado (chopped)
- ½ cup cotija cheese (crumbled)
- ¼ cup tri-color tortilla strips
- ¼ red onion (chopped)
- ¼ teaspoon salt
- ¼ teaspoon pepper

Ingredients for the Avocado Lime Dressing

- 4 tablespoons water
- 1 avocado
- 1 tablespoon mayonnaise
- 1 tablespoon cilantro
- 1 tablespoon extra virgin olive oil
- 1 teaspoon lime juice
- ¼ teaspoon onion powder
- ¼ teaspoon garlic powder
- ¼ teaspoon salt
- ¼ teaspoon pepper
- ⅛ teaspoon sugar or stevia optional

Directions

1. To make the salad, take out a large bowl.

2. Add all the salad ingredients (keep the salt and pepper for last), and then mix them together. Add in the salt and pepper now.

3. For the dressing, take all the ingredients for the dressing and put them in a blender.

4. Run the blender until all the ingredients are smooth.

5. Next take out a plate and then place the salad on it. Take out the dressing and pour it over the salad.

6. Enjoy!

Egg Salad on Lettuce

A little egg salad makes for a light lunch. But what's the best way to make them? Well, you use the recipe below.

Ingredients

- 4 cups fresh lettuce (chopped)
- 3 tablespoons mayonnaise
- 3 large hard-boiled eggs (cooled)
- 1 tablespoon fresh parsley (chopped)
- 1 teaspoon fresh lemon juice
- 1 small stalk celery (diced)

- ¼ teaspoon salt

- ¼ teaspoon pepper

Directions

1. Take out a small bowl. Peel and dice the eggs into it.

2. Add in the celery, mayonnaise, parsley, lemon juice, salt, and pepper. Mix all the ingredients together.

3. Take out a fresh lettuce and place it on a plate. Add the mixture on top of it.

4. Your egg salad is ready to go.

Egg Soup

Sometimes, you might just want to have a little soup during lunch. Or maybe you would like to use the soup along with another dish. Here's your health egg soup ready to go!

Ingredients

- 6 large eggs (whisked)

- 5 cups vegetable broth

- 4 vegetable bouillon cubes

- 1 tablespoons chili garlic paste

- ½ green onion (sliced)

Directions

1. Take out a saucepan and place it over medium heat.

Add the vegetable broth to the saucepan.

2. Crush the bouillon cubes and stir it into the broth in a saucepan.

3. Bring it to a boil, then stir in the chili garlic paste.

4. Cook until steaming, then remove from heat.

5. Take out your whisk and start mixing the broth. As you are whisking it, slowly drizzle in the beaten eggs.

6. Allow the eggs to sit for about 2 minutes then serve with sliced green onion.

Spring Salad Topped with Shaved Parmesan

Most of the salads in this book are easy to make, so you can prep them for a quick bite, including this one that combines the kick of a red wine vinegar and the nuttiness of the parmesan to good effect.

Ingredients

- 4 ounces mixed spring greens
- 2 tablespoons red wine vinegar
- 1 tablespoon Dijon mustard
- ½ small red onion (sliced)
- ¼ teaspoon liquid stevia extract, to taste
- ¼ cup roasted pine nuts

- ¼ cup shaved parmesan

- ¼ teaspoon salt

- ¼ teaspoon pepper

Directions

1. In a small bowl, combine the red wine vinegar and mustard. Whisk them together so they are mixed properly.

2. Add in the salt and pepper. Whisk the dressing a little and then add in the stevia. Whisk again.

3. In another bowl, add spring greens, red onion, pine nuts, and parmesan. Mix them together.

4. Pour the red wine vinegar dressing on top.

Spinach Cauliflower Soup

How about a little healthy soup to make your day? In this soup, we have the twin benefits of spinach and cauliflower mixed with the creaminess of coconut milk.

Ingredients

- 8 ounces fresh baby spinach (chopped)

- 3 cups vegetable broth

- 2 cloves garlic (minced)

- 2 cups chopped cauliflower

- 1 tablespoon coconut oil
- 1 small yellow onion (chopped)
- ½ cup canned coconut milk
- ¼ teaspoon salt
- ¼ teaspoon pepper

Directions

1. Take out a saucepan and place it over medium to high heat. Heat the oil in the saucepan and add the onion and garlic.

2. Sauté for 4-5 minutes until browned, then stir in the cauliflower.

3. Cook for 5 minutes until you see the cauliflower turn brown. Stir in the spinach.

4. Let it cook for 2 minutes until wilted, then stir in the broth and bring it to a boil.

5. Remove the mixture from the heat. Add them all into a blender and then puree the soup. Blend the ingredients until you notice them getting smooth.

6. Stir in the coconut milk, salt, and pepper. Blend again.

7. Transfer to a bowl and enjoy hot.

Spinach and Avocado Salad with Almonds

Do you have even less time than it takes to prepare a salad? Then, we've got a recipe for you that saves time. If you have the ingredients with you, the salad can be prepared anywhere you like.

Ingredients

- 4 cups fresh baby spinach
- 2 tablespoons olive oil
- 1 tablespoons balsamic vinegar
- 1 medium avocado, sliced thinly
- ½ tablespoon Dijon mustard
- ¼ cup sliced almonds (toasted)
- ¼ teaspoon salt
- ¼ teaspoon pepper

Directions

1. Take out a bowl and toss in the spinach along with olive oil, balsamic vinegar, Dijon mustard, salt, and pepper. Make sure you mix them well.

2. You are almost done with the salad.

3. You just have to divide them equally between two plates. Top them off with toasted almonds and avocados.

Quick Chopped Salad (When You Cannot Wait)

What if you are truly in a hurry and would like to shorten the prep time for your salad. Well, you can use the below recipe to dig into a delicious salad even faster than the previous recipe.

Ingredients

- 4 cups fresh chopped lettuce
- 2 hard-boiled eggs (peeled and sliced)
- 1 small avocado (pitted and chopped)
- ½ cup cherry tomatoes (halved)
- ½ cup shredded cheddar cheese
- ¼ cup diced cucumber

Directions

1. Divide the lettuce between two salad plates or bowls.
2. Top the salads with diced avocado, tomato, and celery.
3. Add the sliced egg and shredded cheese.
4. Serve the salads with your favorite keto-friendly dressing.
5. That's all there is to it! Pretty quick isn't it?

Avocado, Lettuce, and Tomato Sandwich

Sometimes, all you need is a nice sandwich for lunch. The avocado and lettuce add the perfect texture to the sandwich while the sweetness of the tomato makes for a wonderful addition. And guess what? We are going to be making the bread in our trusted ovens!

Ingredients

- 1 large egg (separated)
- 1 slice tomato
- 1 ounce cream cheese, softened
- ¼ teaspoon cream of tartar
- ¼ teaspoon salt
- ¼ cup sliced avocado
- ¼ cup shredded lettuce

Directions

1. We will start with the bread first. Preheat the oven to 300°F.

2. Take out a baking tray and line it with parchment paper.

3. In a bowl, beat the egg whites with the cream of tartar and salt until soft peaks form.

4. In a separate bowl, add in cream cheese and egg yolk until smooth and pale yellow. Whisk all the ingredients together.

5. Now take the egg whites and fold them into the second bowl a little at a time until smooth and well combined.

6. Take out the batter using a spoon and spread it around onto the parchment paper into two even circles.

7. Bake for about 25 minutes until you start to notice that the bread has become firm with a light brown color.

8. Take out the bread and finish the preparation by adding in the avocado, lettuce, and tomato.

Artichoke and Spinach Casserole

By adding two different cheese into this dish, you are adding a rich and creamy texture while playing with some incredible flavors. The red pepper is going to add that spicy kick without being too much for your taste buds to handle. After all, we want to tickle your tongue, not burn it!

Ingredients

- 16 large eggs
- 2 cups artichoke hearts
- 2 cups spinach (cleaned and drained well)
- 1 cup white cheddar
- 1 teaspoon salt
- 1 clove garlic (minced)
- ½ cup parmesan cheese
- ½ cup ricotta cheese
- ½ teaspoon dried thyme

- ½ teaspoon crushed red pepper

- ¼ cup onion (chopped)

- ¼ cup milk

Directions

1. Preheat the oven to 350°F. Take out a baking dish and spray it with cooking spray. Crack the eggs into a large bowl and add the milk. Whisk the eggs well to combine.

2. Take another bowl and break the artichoke hearts up into small pieces into it. Separate the leaves. Use paper towels to remove any excess liquid from the spinach.

3. Add both the artichokes and the spinach to the egg mixture. Add all remaining ingredients, except the ricotta cheese, and stir to combine.

4. Pour the mixture into the baking dish.

5. Take out the cheese and spread it evenly over the casserole.

6. Pop the baking dish into the oven and bake for about 30-35 minutes.

7. To test if your casserole has been well cooked, take out the dish and shake it a little. If the center of the dish does not jiggle, then you have yourself a well-cooked casserole!

Shaking Shakshuka!

Shakshuka is a hearty meal that can be enjoyed anytime, even during breakfast or dinner. Even the name itself is fun! Imagine telling someone that you are preparing shakshuka. That will definitely raise the curiosity levels of anyone. Do not worry about the pepper that we are going to add. The sweet marinara sauce will prevent it from getting too hot to handle.

Ingredients

- 4 eggs
- 1 cup marinara sauce
- 1 chili pepper
- 1 teaspoon fresh basil
- ¼ cup feta cheese
- ¼ teaspoon cumin
- ¼ teaspoon salt
- ¼ teaspoon pepper

Directions

1. Start by preheating the oven to about 400°F.

2. Take out a skillet and place it over medium heat. Add the marinara and the pepper into the skillet. Allow the pepper to cook into the marina. This should take about 5 minutes.

3. Crack and gently add your eggs into the marinara sauce.

4. Next, sprinkle feta cheese all over the eggs and season with salt, pepper and cumin. Make sure you spread the cheese evenly over the marinara.

5. Usually, people might ask you to transfer the marinana mixture into a baking tray. But this time, we won't be doing that. We are going to transfer the skillet itself into the oven! Convenient huh?

6. Allow the skillet to remain in the oven for about 10 minutes.

7. Once you notice that the eggs are cooked (but are still runny), take out the skillet from the oven.

8. And that's it! Transfer the dish to a plate and enjoy!

Cheese and Broccoli Fritters

Enjoying fritters does not mean that you have to give up on flavors. It just means that you are going to use some wonderful and healthy ingredients to get incredible results. For this dish, we are going to prepare the dish and a sauce as well!

Ingredients for the Fritters

- 7 tablespoons flaxseed meal
- 2 large eggs
- 2 teaspoons baking powder
- ¾ cup almond flour

- ½ cup mozzarella cheese
- ½ cup fresh broccoli
- ¼ teaspoon salt
- ¼ teaspoon pepper

Ingredients for the Sauce
- ½ tablespoon lemon juice
- ¼ cup mayonnaise
- ¼ cup fresh chopped dill
- ¼ teaspoon salt
- ¼ teaspoon pepper

Directions

1. Take out a food processor and add in the broccoli. Blend until you see it getting smooth.

2. Put the blended broccoli into a bowl. Mix together the cheese, almond flour, 4 tablespoons flaxseed meal and baking powder with the broccoli.

3. Add the 2 eggs and mix all the ingredients together well until everything is mixed well.

4. Roll the batter into balls. Coat with a little flaxseed meal. Continue doing this with the remaining batter. You can use a paper towel to hold all the batter.

5. Time to get out your deep fryer. Preheat it to around 375°F.

6. Take out the basket and place the broccoli and cheese fritters inside it. Make sure that you are not crowding it too much.

7. Fry the fritters until golden brown, about 3-5 minutes.

Stuffed Zucchini with Marinara

Making a stuffed zucchini is not complicated, as you will notice from this dish. The best part is that you can actually prepare them for your friends or family and show off your cooking skills.

Ingredients

- 4 medium-sized zucchini
- 1-½ cups marinara sauce
- ½ cup goat cheese
- 1 teaspoon chopped parsley

Directions

1. Preheat the oven to 400°F.

2. Slice the zucchini in half lengthwise and scoop out the seeds, leaving the zucchini hollowed out.

3. Line up a baking tray with sheet and then place the zucchini on top of it.

4. Season with kosher salt and freshly ground black pepper.

5. Using half of the goat cheese that you have with you, spread a small amount in the bottom of each zucchini.

6. Spoon marinara sauce on top. Sprinkle the remaining goat cheese evenly on top of the sauce.

7. Place the baking tray in the oven then bake the zucchini until goat cheese is soft and marinara is bubbling.

8. This usually takes about 10 minutes.

9. You are ready to eat your zucchini or show off your skills to others.

Cauliflower Steak Take

One of the changes you start noticing on the keto diet is the fact that if you did not like cauliflower before, you just begin to enjoy it now because of the variety of ways in which you can cook them. If you already liked cauliflower before, then this recipe is going to create a newfound love for the vegetable.

Ingredients

- 4 tablespoons butter
- 2 tablespoons seasoning blend (get your favorite one)
- 1 large head cauliflower
- 1 teaspoon salt

- ¼ cup parmesan cheese

- ¼ teaspoon pepper

Directions

1. Preheat the oven to 400°F.

2. If the cauliflower that you bought has leaves on it, then remove them.

3. Slice the cauliflower lengthwise, starting from the top and slicing all the way through the core. Using this method, make slices of cauliflowers that are ideally 1 inch thick.

4. Melt butter inside a microwave. Take it out and add the seasoning to it. Make a paste out of the butter.

5. Using a brush, coat the cauliflowers with the spiced butter.

6. Sprinkle with salt and pepper.

7. Place a nonstick pan over medium heat. Place the cauliflower steaks on the pan and cook them for about 2-3 minutes or until they turn a shade of light brown.

8. Once one side is browned, flip over the steaks and cook the other side.

9. Take out a baking tray and line it with a sheet. Place the cauliflowers on the baking sheet.

10. Pop the tray into the over and bake the cauliflowers for about 15-20 minutes.

11. Take it out of the oven, sprinkle with some parmesan cheese and serve while hot.

Limey Creamy Coleslaw

This coleslaw is the perfect accompaniment to any of the dinner dishes that you have seen here. But if you are in the mood for something light, then you can have this on your own. The trick to this dish is the lime and the kick that it adds to all the flavors.

Ingredients

- 2 limes (juiced)
- 1-½ cups coleslaw
- 1-½ avocados
- 1 garlic clove
- 1 teaspoon cilantro
- ½ teaspoon salt
- ¼ cup cilantro leaves
- ¼ cup water

Directions

1. In a food processor add the garlic and cilantro and blend them together until chopped.

2. Add the lime juice, avocados, and water. Continue blending until everything is nice and creamy.

3. Take out the avocado mixture, and in a large bowl, mix it with the coleslaw. It will be a bit thick, but it will cover the slaw nicely.

4. For best results, refrigerate for a few hours before eating to soften the cabbage.

Cauliflower Hummus

Think about some of the dinner recipes right here. Wouldn't it be better if there was some kind of dip or sauce to go along with it? Your wish has been answered.

Ingredients

- 3 cups raw cauliflower florets
- 3 whole garlic cloves
- 3 tablespoons extra virgin olive oil
- 3 tablespoons lemon juice
- 2 tablespoons water
- 2 raw garlic cloves (crushed – these are additional garlic cloves that will be used separately)
- 2 tablespoons extra virgin olive oil
- 1-½ tablespoons tahini paste
- ¾ teaspoon kosher salt

- ½ teaspoon smoked paprika

Directions

1. Take out a dish that is microwave safe and then combine the cauliflower, water, 2 tablespoons of olive oil, about ½ teaspoon of kosher salt, and the 3 whole garlic cloves.

2. Place the bowl into a microwave for about 15 minutes or until softened and darkened in color.

3. Put the cauliflower mixture into a blender and let the machine run. Add the tahini paste, lemon juice, 2 raw garlic cloves, 3 tablespoons of olive oil, and the remaining kosher salt. Blend them all together until they look smooth. If you would like to add more flavors, taste the puree and make adjustments.

4. To serve, place the hummus in a bowl and drizzle with extra virgin olive oil and a sprinkle of paprika. Use thinly sliced tart apples, celery sticks, raw radish chips, or other veggies to dip with.

The Greek Wrapper

We are going to take a trip to Greek to wrap ourselves in their cuisine (no pun intended). Let's check out a unique way to have your veggies.

Ingredients for the Wrap

- 8 whole kalamata olives (halved)

- 4 large cherry tomatoes (halved)

- 4 large collard green leaves (washed)
- 1 medium cucumber (sliced)
- ½ medium red bell pepper (sliced)
- ½ cup purple onion (diced)
- ½ block feta (cut into strips)

Ingredients for the Tzatziki Sauce

- 2 tablespoons olive oil
- 2 tablespoons minced fresh dill
- 1 cup full-fat plain Greek yogurt
- 1 teaspoon garlic powder
- 1 tablespoon white vinegar
- ¼ cup cucumber (seeded and grated)
- ¼ teaspoon salt
- ¼ teaspoon pepper

Directions

1. Take out a bowl and mix all the ingredients for the tzatziki sauce together. Once they are mixed, store in the fridge. Be sure to squeeze all the water out of the cucumber after you grate it.

2. Now we are going to prepare collard green wraps. We

start off by washing the leaves well and trimming the fibrous stem from each leaf.

3. Spread 2 tablespoons of tzatziki onto the center of each wrap and spread the sauce around.

4. Add the cucumber, pepper, onion, olives, feta, and tomatoes in the center of the wrap.

5. Fold the wrap like you are folding a burrito. If you haven't folded a burrito before, then don't worry! Here is how you do it. You start off by folding each side toward the center. You then fold the rounded end over the filling and roll.

6. And that's it! You can slice the wrap in halves and serve with any leftover tzatziki or wrap in plastic for a quick lunchtime meal!

Egg Drop and Zucchini Soup

This soup comes with a nice little surprise. It's got noodles! In fact, you might not believe what these noodles are made from. The entire dish is hearty, filling, and just oozing with that nice minced garlic flavor.

Ingredients

- 8 cups vegetable broth (divided)
- 5 cups shiitake mushrooms (sliced)
- 5 tablespoons low-sodium soy sauce
- 4 medium to large zucchinis

- 4 large eggs (beaten)
- 3 tablespoons cornstarch
- 2 tablespoons extra virgin olive oil
- 2 cups water (divided into 1 cup)
- 2 tablespoons minced ginger
- 2 cups thinly sliced scallions (divided)
- ½ teaspoons red pepper flakes
- ½ teaspoons salt
- ½ teaspoons pepper

Directions

1. The first thing that we have to do is create zucchini noodles. We are going to first cut the tops off the zucchini. Then, cut the zucchini into two halves.

2. Next, we are going to run the zucchini through a spiralizer. Once you do that, you have yourself some really cool noodles! Wait, you thought we were going to use store bought noodles? No way!

3. In a large pot, heat the olive oil over medium-high heat.

4. Add the minced ginger and cook, stirring, for 2 minutes.

5. Add the shiitake mushrooms and a tablespoon of water and cook until the mushrooms begin to sweat.

6. Add 7 cups of the vegetable broth, the remaining water, the red pepper flakes, tamari sauce, and 1-½ cups of chopped scallions. Bring to a boil, stirring occasionally.

7. Meanwhile, mix the remaining cup of vegetable broth with the cornstarch and whisk until completely smooth.

8. While stirring the soup, slowly pour in the beaten eggs in a thin stream. Continue stirring until all of the egg is incorporated.

9. Slowly pour the cornstarch mixture into the soup and cook for about 4-5 minutes to thicken.

10. Season to taste with salt and pepper (usually I add just a bit of pepper, but as long as I'm using a full-sodium vegetable broth, I don't need any extra salt).

11. Add the spiralized zucchini noodles to the pot and cook, stirring, for about 2 minutes, or until the noodles are just soft and flexible (remember, they'll continue cooking in your bowl!).

12. Serve topped with the remaining scallions.

13. Who would have thought noodles could be made from zucchini right?

Veggie Red Curry

Ever heard of Thai red curry? Have you ever tried it? Well, welcome to the world of the veggie red curry. Oh and it will still include the coconut flavor so popular with traditional red curries.

Ingredients

- 4 tablespoons coconut oil
- 2 teaspoons soy sauce
- 1 cup broccoli florets
- 1 teaspoon minced garlic
- 1 tablespoon red curry paste
- 1 teaspoon minced ginger
- 1 large handful of spinach
- ½ cup coconut cream (or coconut milk)
- ¼ medium onion

Directions

1. Place a pan on medium heat and add about 2 tablespoons of the oil into it.

2. When the oil is hot, add the onion to the pan and let it sizzle. Allow it to cook for 3-4 minutes to caramelize and become semi-translucent.

3. Once this happens, add the garlic to the pan and let it brown slightly. This typically takes around 30 seconds.

4. Turn the heat to medium-low and add broccoli florets to the pan. Stir everything together well. Let the broccoli take on the flavors of the onion and garlic. This

should take about 1-2 minutes.

5. Move everything in your pan to the side and add 1 tablespoon red curry paste. You want this hitting the bottom of the pan so that all the flavors can be released from the spices.

6. Once your red curry paste starts to smell pungent, mix everything together again and add a large handful of spinach over the top.

7. Allow the spinach to wilt a little. Once it has done that, add the coconut milk into the dish and mix everything well.

8. Stir everything together and then add the remaining 2 tablespoons of coconut oil, 2 tablespoons soy sauce, and minced ginger. Let all the ingredients simmer for 5-10 minutes, depending on how thick you want the sauce.

9. That's it. Take out the dish and serve. You can easily compliment the red curry with the fritters' recipe that was mentioned earlier.

Chapter 5: Delectable Dinner Goodness

Dinnertime is all about sitting down in front of a delicious meal. You can choose to have the meal by itself or while watching your favorite movie.

The important thing is that you are having something that not only fills your stomach until the next day, but does not make you feel bloated (which is not something you want to experience right before you go to bed).

Below, you are going to some carefully selected dinner recipes that can go well on their own or along with your favorite smoothie recipe from Chapter 3.

Onwards to wonderful dinner secrets and tasteful dishes.

Baked Mushrooms, Italian Style

Everyone loves some mushrooms. So let's bring in the flavors of Italy into this dish that really look simple to prepare but has so much going on with it. The end result – something beautiful to look at and delicious to dig into.

Ingredients

- 4 Portobello mushrooms

- 2 tablespoons ghee

- 2 tablespoons fresh basil

- 1 cup grated parmesan cheese

- 1 large can tomatoes (unsweetened)
- 1 tablespoon fresh parsley
- 1 teaspoon dried oregano
- ¼ teaspoon salt (2 spoons of ¼ each – 1 for the mushrooms and 1 later for the canned tomatoes)
- ¼ teaspoon pepper

Directions

1. Preheat the oven to 400°F.
2. Next, clean the mushrooms and slice them however you like.
3. Take out a nonstick pan and place it over medium heat. Add in your ghee into the pan.
4. Toss in your mushrooms into the pan and season it with your salt and pepper. Mix everything and allow the ingredients to cook for about 5 minutes.
5. Take out a baking tray and place the mushrooms inside them.
6. Wash the basil, parsley, and organo. Chop them up well.
7. In a bowl, add canned tomatoes and layer it with the herbs you just chopped. Add the remaining salt into the dish.
8. Top it all off with your grated parmesan.

9. Place your baking tray into the oven for about 25 minutes.

10. After that, take it out and place it on a cooling rack or any other surface to cool for about a couple of minutes.

Spinach Ricotta Bake

Why not go crazy for some ricotta? And while you are at it, why not add in two more types of cheese to get the cheesiest party started on your taste buds (no pun intended again)?

Ingredients

- 4 cups frozen spinach

- 2 eggs

- 2 cups ricotta

- 1 garlic clove (finely chopped)

- 1 tablespoon extra virgin olive oil

- 1 teaspoon sprinkle of organic broth granules

- ½ teaspoon alt

- ½ teaspoon nutmeg

- ½ teaspoon paprika

- ½ teaspoon pepper

- ½ cup mozzarella

- ¼ cup double cream
- ¼ cup parmesan

Directions

1. Take out a wok and place it over medium to high heat. Add in the olive oil.

2. Add spinach, garlic, broth granules, pepper, nutmeg, and paprika.

3. Stir and cook until the ingredients look dry. Set aside the wok to cool.

4. Preheat oven to 400°F.

5. Now take the eggs into a bowl and whisk them.

6. Add ricotta and whisk again. Add the cream and continue whisking.

7. Add ¼ salt, the spinach from the wok (which should be cooled by now), half of the parmesan, and all the mozzarella.

8. Stir everything together. Now take out a baking tray and layer the ingredients into it.

9. Use a spoon to make the surface even. Add the remaining parmesan evenly on top.

10. Bake for about 40-50 minutes or until the top layer takes on a brown coating.

11. Once done, take out the dish and serve.

White Egg Pizza

If you are planning a pizza party, forget getting them from the local chain where you are most probably going to be digging into a lot of fat and grease. Try this healthy option instead.

Ingredients

- 2 tablespoons extra virgin olive oil
- 2 tablespoons egg fast alfredo sauce
- 2 large eggs
- 2 tablespoons monterey jack cheese (shredded)
- 1 tablespoon water
- 1 tablespoon green onion (chopped)
- ½ teaspoon cumin
- ½ teaspoon kosher salt
- ½ teaspoon pepper
- ½ pickled jalapeno (minced)

Directions

1. Begin by preheating oven to 350°F.

2. Take out a pan and place it over medium to high heat. Add in the olive oil. Spread the oil around to

the sides of the pan as well as best as you can.

3. Add cumin, kosher salt, and pepper to the eggs in a bowl. Add the water and beat until frothy using a fork or a whisk.

4. Pour the eggs the pan and cook them until eggs are set on the bottom.

5. You might notice that the top might look a little wobbly. But that is okay! They will still be a little moist and wobbly on top.

6. Add the egg fast alfredo sauce and half of the chopped pickled jalapeno. Add shredded cheese and green onion. Mix them all well.

7. Now transfer the pan itself into the oven, preferably on the top rack.

8. Bake for about 3-5 minutes.

9. Take it out and enjoy!

Roasted Mushrooms with Feta, Herbs, and Red Pepper

Everyone loves some mushrooms. So let's bring in the flavors of Italy into this dish that really looks simple to prepare but has so much going on with it. The end result; – something beautiful to look at and delicious to dig into.

Ingredients

- 12 ounces of jar-roasted red pepper (drained and chopped into small pieces)

- 4 tablespoons extra virgin olive oil

- 3 tablespoons fresh lemon juice

- 2 tablespoons fresh mint (chopped)

- 2 tablespoons fresh oregano (chopped)

- 2 cups fresh brown mushrooms

- ½ teaspoon salt

- ½ teaspoon pepper

- ¼ cup feta cheese

Directions

1. Begin by preheating the oven to 450°F. Take out a roasting pan and line it with aluminum foil.

2. Take a small bowl and mix about 2 tablespoons of the olive oil, lemon juice, red pepper, mint, and oregano. Mix all the ingredients well and then set them aside to marinate.

3. Wash the mushrooms and then cut them into quarters.

4. Cut large mushrooms into quarters. Take another bowl and add in the mushrooms, the remaining 2 tablespoons of oil, salt, and pepper.

5. Arrange the mushrooms on the roasting pan. Pop the pan into the oven.

6. Let the mushrooms roast for about 15 minutes or until mushrooms are starting to get brown.

7. Take out the pan, turn the mushrooms over and then roast them for about 5 minutes more. At this point, the mushrooms should be brown all over. If not, then place them into the oven and roast again for another 3 minutes.

8. Place the mushrooms back into the bowl that you took them out of. Add in the red pepper mixture into the bowl and mix well.

9. Arrange the mushrooms on a plate. Sprinkle the feta cheese on top, and serve.

Eggplant Hash, The Moroccon Way

More hash for you, but this time, we are going to try it out in a Moroccan style. Sounds adventurous? Then let's get started.

Ingredients

- 4 garlic cloves (minced)
- 2 tablespoons ghee

- 2 small red bell peppers (seeded and cubed)
- 1 large eggplant (peeled, cubed and salted)
- 1 medium red onion (diced)
- ½ teaspoon ground cinnamon
- ½ teaspoon coriander seed
- ½ teaspoon cayenne powder
- ½ teaspoon salt
- ½ teaspoon pepper
- ¼ cup slivered almonds (toasted)
- ½ cup sun-dried tomatoes
- ¼ cup fresh mint leaves

Directions

1. Pre-heat a really large sauté pan or wok over high heat. Add your oil and swirl it around to coat the pan. Quickly add your eggplant and peppers. Add salt and pepper.

2. Toss the veggies in the pan to coat with the oil, then allow them to sit in the pan and sear for about 1 minute. Make sure they are evenly spread on the bottom of the pan and not piled up in one part.

Toss them and spread them out to sear for another minute.

3. After about 2 to 3 minutes, add your onions and garlic, then toss the ingredients together and allow them to sit for about 2 more minutes. Season with a little salt and pepper and then toss and spread and then allow the veggies to sear for another minute or two.

4. Add your almonds, sun-dried tomatoes, and fresh mint leaves. Mix the ingredients well. You are only looking to heat up the new ingredients. They don't need any further cooking.

5. Taste your hash. If it needs a little more salt and pepper, add it. Finally, sprinkle the spices on top of all the ingredients, mix everything together.

6. Serve while hot!

Falafel with Tahini Sauce

This Middle Eastern delight is a vegetarian's dream come true. You might also find them added to sandwiches or wraps. But this time, we are going to enjoy them by themselves, with a generous helping of tahini sauce.

Ingredients for the Falafel

- 3 tablespoons coconut flour

- 2 tablespoons fresh parsley (chopped)

- 2 large eggs
- 1 cup raw cauliflower (pureed)
- 1 teaspoon kosher salt
- 1 tablespoon ground cumin
- 1 tablespoon olive oil
- 1 clove garlic (minced)
- ½ cup ground slivered almonds
- ½ tablespoon ground coriander
- ½ teaspoon cayenne pepper

Ingredients for Tahini sauce
- 3 tablespoons water
- 2 tablespoons tahini paste
- 1 tablespoon lemon juice
- 1 clove garlic (minced)
- ½ teaspoon salt

Directions
1. Firstly, chop up the cauliflower and then add it to the blender. Run the machine until all the

ingredients are blended together and the mixture turns smooth.

2. Add in the almonds as well but make sure that you do not over grind them, you want the crunchy texture to remain.

3. Take out a medium bowl and then combine the ground cauliflower and ground almonds. Add the rest of the ingredients and mix them really well.

4. Take out a pan and place it on medium heat. Add in the olive oil and heat up. While it's heating, take the ground cauliflower mix and create 8 patties that are 3 inches wide.

5. Fry them four at a time until browned on one side and then flip and cook the other side. Once they are done, transfer them to a plate.

6. For the tahini sauce, simply combine all the ingredients in a blender and blend them until they are smooth.

7. Serve the dish with tahini sauce.

Asparagus Quiche

When it is time to make some quick quiches, then nothing comes close to this receipt. The parmesan and mozzarella just compliment the spinach and asparagus that goes into the dish.

Ingredients

- 8 ounces asparagus (cooked)
- 6 eggs (beaten)
- 2-½ cup mozzarella cheese (grated)
- 2 cups baby spinach leaves
- 2 tablespoons parmesan cheese (grated)
- 2 cloves garlic (minced)
- ½ teaspoon salt
- ½ teaspoon pepper

Directions

1. Preheat the oven to about 375°F.
2. Take out a pie pan and lightly grease it with cooking spray.
3. Combine eggs with 2 cups of grated mozzarella cheese and garlic in a bowl. Mix them all together well.
4. Take out about ¼ of the egg mixture and set it aside for now.
5. In the remaining egg mixture, stir spinach leaves and pour into the prepared pan. Layer asparagus

on top of egg mixture in pan.

6. Take out the ¼ egg mixture that you had set aside and then pour the mixture on top of the asparagus.

7. Add remaining mozzarella and all the parmesan cheese on top.

8. Pop the pie pan into the oven and bake for about 30 minutes or until you notice the edges start to turn brown.

Mediterranean Pasta

The Mediterranean conjures up images of the sun, beaches, and clear waters. Get ready to bring those images to life with this pasta recipe.

Ingredients

- 10 kalamata olives (halved)
- 5 cloves garlic (minced)
- 2 large zucchinis (cut using spiralizer)
- 2 tablespoons olive oil
- 2 tablespoons capers
- 2 tablespoons parsley (chopped)
- 2 tablespoons butter

- 1 cup spinach (packed)
- ½ teaspoon salt
- ½ teaspoon pepper
- ¼ cup sun-dried tomatoes
- ¼ cup parmesan cheese (shredded)
- ¼ cup feta cheese (crumbled)

Directions

1. Take out a large pan and place it over medium heat. Add zucchini, spinach, olive oil, butter, garlic, salt, and pepper. Sauté until zucchini is tender and spinach is wilted. Drain excess liquid.

2. To the pan, add sun-dried tomatoes, capers, parsley, and kalamata olives. Mix in and sauté for 2-3 minutes.

3. Remove from heat and toss all the ingredients with parmesan and feta cheeses before serving.

Cheesy Risotto

This risotto oozes with all the cheesy goodness. What makes it standout is the added flavor of Dijon mustard that brings out the flavors of all the ingredients in the dish.

Ingredients

- 3 tablespoons freshly chopped chives
- 1 medium cauliflower
- 1 small white onion (chopped)
- 1 cup vegetable stock
- 1 teaspoon Dijon mustard
- 1 cup cheddar cheese (shredded)
- 1 cup parmesan cheese (grated)
- ½ teaspoon salt
- ½ teaspoon pepper
- ¼ cup ghee

Directions

1. We are going to make the cauliflower rice first. If the cauliflower has leaves, then remove them first and put them in a food processor. You are not going to make a smooth paste out of it. Rather, you are going to process the cauliflower into tiny bits.

2. Once you have done that, take out a large pan and place it over medium heat. Grease the pan with ghee or butter. Once hot, add the finely chopped onion and cook until lightly browned.

3. Add in the cauliflower rice and mix all the ingredients well.

4. Cook for just a few minutes and pour in the vegetable stock. Cook for another 5 minutes or until the cauli-rice is tender. Meanwhile, grate the cheddar and parmesan cheese.

5. Add the mustard into the pan, stir the ingredients, and take off the heat.

6. Add the grated cheese and mix well. Keep some parmesan cheese for garnish. Add the freshly chopped chives and also keep some for garnish. Add the salt and pepper.

7. Finally, place the risotto into serving bowls and top with the remaining parmesan cheese and chives.

Chapter 6: Tasteful Snacks and Desserts

It is time to hit the sweet spot! What better way to do it than by indulging in some sweet goodness and lip smacking snacks that will make you wonder, "Why didn't I try this before?"

Cauliflower with Tzatziki Dip

Enjoy cauliflowers? Then why not compliment them with a dip?

Ingredients

- 2 cups cauliflower florets
- 2 tablespoons chives (chopped)
- 1 cup sour cream
- 1 tablespoon ranch seasoning
- 1 cucumber (diced)
- ½ package cream cheese

Directions

1. Take out the electric mixer.

2. Add the cream cheese into it and beat it until it looks smooth and creamy. You can also beat it manually if you like.

3. Add in the ranch seasoning and sour cream, then continue beating it for a couple of minutes.

4. Add in the chives and cucumbers. Place it in the refrigerator for at least half an hour before serving.

Macadamia Nuts Roasted in Curry

Enjoy curry so much that you are wondering if you can make something quickly without having to resort to a complex dish? You wish has been granted. This crunchy dish can be eaten with any lunch or dinner recipe.

Ingredients

- 2 cups macadamia nuts (preferably raw)
- 1-½ tablespoons olive oil
- 1 tablespoon curry powder
- ½ teaspoon salt

Directions

1. Preheat the oven to 300°F. Take out a baking tray and line it with parchment.

2. Whisk together the olive oil, curry powder, and salt in a mixing bowl.

3. Toss in the macadamia nuts to coat, then spread it on the baking sheet.

4. Bake for 25 minutes until toasted, then cool to

room temperature.

Chia and Coconut Pudding

The best part of the pudding is that you can enjoy them anytime. This pudding can be placed in the refrigerator and you can have it whenever you feel like enjoying a delightful snack.

Ingredients

- 2-¼ cup canned coconut milk
- 1 teaspoon vanilla extract
- 1 teaspoon liquid stevia
- ½ teaspoon salt
- ½ cup chia seeds

Directions

1. Take out a bowl and combine the coconut milk, vanilla, and salt.
2. Stir well and sweeten with stevia.
3. Whisk in the chia seeds and chill overnight.
4. Spoon into bowls and serve with chopped nuts or fruit.

Lemon Meringue Cookies

A little sweetness and plenty of lemon zest-ness to make this cookie a fan favorite.

Ingredients

- 4 Egg Whites
- 1 teaspoon liquid stevia
- ½ teaspoon lemon extract
- ¼ teaspoon salt

Directions

1. Preheat the oven to 225°F.
2. Take out a baking tray and line it with baking sheet.
3. Place the egg whites in a bowl. Beat them until they turn smooth and frothy.
4. Add in the salt and keep whisking them until peaks form.
5. Add the lemon extract into the egg whites and then continue to whisk for a little while longer.
6. Finally, transfer the mixture into a piping bag.
7. Pipe that into the baking sheet and then pop the tray into the oven.

8. Bake for 45 minutes. Once done, turn off the oven and let the cookies cool inside for about 1-2 hours.

9. You can either have them immediately or store them for the next day.

Cinnamon Bread

There is something about having a sweet and spicy combination of cinnamon bread. You can actually combine the bread with the brownie recipe that we just saw.

Ingredients

- 6 tablespoons canned coconut milk
- 3 tablespoons melted coconut oil
- 3 large eggs (whisked)
- 2 tablespoons water
- 1-¼ teaspoon ground cinnamon
- 1 teaspoon baking soda
- 1 teaspoon apple cider vinegar
- 1 teaspoon liquid stevia
- ½ cup coconut flour
- ½ teaspoon salt

- ¼ teaspoon baking powder

Directions

1. Preheat the oven to 350°F. Take out a loaf pan and grease it lightly with cooking spray.

2. Combine the coconut flour, cinnamon, baking soda, baking powder, and salt in a mixing bowl and stir well.

3. In another bowl, whisk together the coconut milk, oil, water, vinegar, and eggs.

4. Stir the wet ingredients into the dry, then sweeten to taste with stevia.

5. Spread the batter in the pan and cook for 25 to 30 minutes, then let cool.

Coconut Macaroons

I like to think of macaroons as delightful little cookies. But how can you make one that stays true to the macaroon spirit and still manages to be unique? You do this by this recipe.

Ingredients

- 3 large egg whites

- 2 tablespoons powdered erythritol

- 1 tablespoon coconut oil

- 1 teaspoon vanilla extract

- ½ cup unsweetened shredded coconut
- ½ teaspoon coconut extract
- ¼ cup almond flour

Directions

1. Preheat the oven to 400°F. Take out a baking tray and line it with parchment.
2. Combine the almond flour, coconut, and erythritol in a bowl. Mix them well.
3. In a separate bowl, add the coconut oil, then whisk in the extracts (vanilla and coconut).
4. Stir the mixtures from the first and second bowl together
5. Beat the egg whites in a bowl until stiff peaks form, then fold into the batter.
6. Spoon onto the baking sheet in even-sized mounds.
7. Bake for 7-9 minutes until the macaroons are just browned on the edges.

Vanilla Ice Cream with Coconut

This comfort food comes with the delightful flavor of coconut. And if you are wondering if it's difficult to make? Then worry not.

Ingredients

- 2 cups canned coconut milk (divided)
- 1 tablespoon coconut oil
- 1 teaspoon vanilla extract
- ½ teaspoon liquid stevia

Directions

1. Take out a saucepan and place it over medium heat. Add the coconut oil in it. Then whisk in half of the coconut milk.

2. Bring to a boil, then reduce heat and simmer for 30 minutes.

3. Pour into a bowl and sweeten with stevia, then let cool to room temperature.

4. Stir in the vanilla extract, then pour the remaining coconut milk into a bowl.

5. Beat the coconut milk until stiff peaks form, then fold into the other mixture.

6. Spoon into a loaf pan and freeze until firm.

Ginger Cookies

Why add ginger as a small part of the meal when it can be the main component of it? Presenting, the ginger cookies!

Ingredients

- 1 cup coconut butter
- 1 large egg
- 1 teaspoon vanilla extract
- ½ cup powdered erythritol
- ½ teaspoon ground ginger
- ½ teaspoon baking soda
- ¼ teaspoon ground nutmeg
- ¼ teaspoon salt

Directions

1. Preheat the oven to 350°F. Take out a baking tray and line lit with parchment.

2. Place the coconut butter in a food processor with the egg and vanilla.

3. Blend until it becomes smooth then add the erythritol, ginger, baking soda, nutmeg, and salt.

4. Pulse until it forms a dough, then shape into 16 small balls.

5. Place the balls on the baking sheet and flatten slightly.

Bake for 12-15 minutes until the edges are browned then cool.

Conclusion

Finally, we are at the end of our journey.

But that does not mean your personal journey has ended.

The hardest part about keto is not starting it, but maintaining it. This is why you should never give into peer pressure. Do not easily be tempted by sugar-rich and carb-rich foods. Stay true to your journey because at the end of it, you will gain incredible benefits.

Most importantly, do not forget to exercise.

That's right! Just because you are on a keto diet does not mean that you can to skip your workout routines.

When you are heading into a better lifestyle, you are not only focusing on what you eat, but how well you take care of your body as well.

Getting regular exercise is important. Not staying in one position for too long is also important.

With that, I wish you good look on the road to a healthier tomorrow.

Stay healthy!

www.ingramcontent.com/pod-product-compliance
Lightning Source LLC
LaVergne TN
LVHW091700070526
838199LV00050B/2229